Karen Rudnick, Anne P. Copeland and Helenann Wright

WELCOME TO
BOSTON

A Guide for
International Newcomers

Seventeenth Edition

The Interchange Institute

Table of Contents

Important
Documents

Here are some sites from the US government that you may find helpful:

travel.state.gov
www.state.gov/travel
www.state.gov/business
www.uscis.gov
www.ssa.gov

The **Student and Exchange Visitor Information System (SEVIS)** is a database for international students and scholars. Every US college and university is required to tell the federal government about its international students, including (but not limited to):

- demographic data (like name, citizenship, birth date, field of study),
- some changes in course of study, and
- change of address or name.

Students should check with their international student or scholars office to be sure they understand what rules apply to them. To learn more:

www.ice.gov/sevis

Documents You Will Need

Having the right documents is very important, yet there are many complicated rules about different kinds of visas. Be sure you understand the rules that apply to you. Students should work directly with their International Student/Scholar Office at their university to be sure they comply with the law. Here is some very general information:

Documents

- Keep your passport, visa, and all certification and arrival-departure records in a safe place at all times. You may need your passport as you settle into your housing in Boston, as identification. After that, do not carry it with you around town but rather, keep it in a safe place.
- Make a photocopy of these documents and keep the copies in a separate safe place.
- Be sure you understand the rules that apply to you concerning a Social Security card, a driver's license, taxes, and immunizations.
- When you travel outside the US, be sure you understand any restrictions that apply to you about re-entering. For example, students may need to have a signature from their international student advisor on Form I-20.

Visa

Your visa may allow you to work in the US. Some students are only allowed to work on campus and/or after they have been in the US for more than one year. Others are allowed to work only if it is part of their curriculum (for example, if an internship is required for a degree). Check with your International Student/Scholar Office for help in knowing whether you are allowed to work.

Regardless of your spouse's visa status, you may be able to get a visa that allows you to work based on your own credentials and skills. If you are interested in changing your visa status during your stay in the US, consult an immigration lawyer, who can explain the procedures to you.

Social Security Card

If you are allowed to work in the US you will need a Social Security card, issued by the US government. This number is also used as identification when applying for bank accounts, buying a car, or getting a driver's license. Go to a Social Security office and begin your application process as soon as you arrive in the area. Your application will be coordinated with the federal government, which can take as long as 8 weeks. Ask the Social Security office for a letter stating that you have applied for a Social Security number. This letter may be sufficient for some identification purposes.

Dependents may need an Individual Taxpayer Identification Number (ITIN) instead of a Social Security number. ITINs are given to foreign nationals who have federal tax reporting or filing requirements but do not qualify for a Social Security number. See **www.irs.gov/individuals/ individual-taxpayer-identification-number #what** for details and a list of places to get help with this process.

International Student/Scholar Offices can help advise students about whether they can or must have a Social Security card, and the location of the nearest office to campus.

Your Address

You are required by law to register your address

Your Social Security Card

The Boston Social Security office is located at:
O'Neill Federal Building
Room 135 (1st floor)
10 Causeway Street
Boston, MA 02222
telephone: (800) 772-1213

Hours: Monday-Tuesday 9-4
Wednesday 9-12
Thursday-Friday 9-4

Or go to this site: www. socialsecurity.gov/locator and enter your zipcode to find the office closest to you.

You will need to submit an application, which you can get at the office, or can download from:
www.socialsecurity.gov/ online/ss-5.html

Be sure to bring with you documents that prove your age, identity, and visa status.

See this site for publications on a wide range of Social Security topics: www.ssa. gov/pubs/

Bringing a Pet Into the US

If you are bringing a pet with you into the US, consult the US Department of Agriculture (USDA) website:

/www.aphis.usda.gov/aphis/pet-travel/pet-travel-homepage

and the Centers for Disease Control (CDC) website:

www.cdc.gov/importation/bringing-an-animal-into-the-united-states/index.html

for information on what documents are needed.

with the US government while living in the US. If you move, you must also register the new address. Students register their moves through their International Student/Scholar Office. Others must file on line or with Form AR-11 within 10 days of their move. Go to **www.uscis.gov/ar-11** to learn if you can file on line or to download the form.

When you open some accounts (like at a bank or the public library), you may be asked for proof of your local address. A signed lease (or *purchase and sale agreement* if you have bought a home) is the most official form of proof. However, they may accept an envelope that has been mailed to you, with a cancelled stamp. For example, a utility bill, or in some cases, even a personal letter, may be enough proof.

Massachusetts ID

If you do not plan to get a Massachusetts driver's license, you may still want to get an official Massachusetts identification (ID) card. It will serve as official identification, showing your birth date and your photograph. Apply at any full service Registry of Motor Vehicles (see *Traveling Around Town* chapter) or go to their web site: **www.massrmv. com**

Student Identification (ID) Card

Students will probably be issued a student ID card. This is a valuable card, as it will allow you to use the university facilities (libraries, computer centers, sports facilities, etc) and may allow you to use those of some neighboring universities as well. In addition, you will be able to get discount prices all over the city and US at some stores, theaters, museums, the T, and more. Do not be shy about asking, "Do you have a special student discount price?"

Finding a Place to Live

Picking a Home

Some questions to ask yourself:

- How will I get to work/school from here?

- Am I comfortable in this neighborhood?

- Does this building seem secure? Does the door lock securely? If there are windows on the first floor, are there bars? Do I feel safe if there are no bars? Is the water pressure okay? (It's okay to test the sinks and shower.)

- Where will I study/work?

- Is there parking for me and/or guests? Is the parking on or offstreet? Indoor or outside?

- Is there enough storage?

- Does the kitchen have a refrigerator? (Landlords are not required to provide them although many do.)

- Is this kitchen comfortable for me?

- Is there a place to do laundry in the building? If not, where is the nearest laundromat?

- If I have children, where will they go to school and how will they get there from here?

- Are utilities such as electricity, gas, heating and/or air conditioning included in the rent? If not, what are they likely to cost?

- When can I move in?

Choosing Where to Live

One of your first jobs is to decide where in Boston you would like to live. Students who want to live off campus may be able to get help from their school's housing office, which maintains apartment listings for landlords and real estate agents who rent to students. For each community, area, or home you are considering, ask yourself the following questions:

Being Near Where You Need to Go. How far away from your school/work will you be? While many people try to live as close as possible, others choose to live further away from the city where they can find more affordable housing. In any case, consider how you will get there. Can you walk there safely? Can you walk there comfortably on snowy winter days? Will you be close to public transportation? How long will the trip to school/work take? Will you need a car? If so, is there parking nearby (both at home and at work/school)? Many communities in Boston have strict parking restrictions and/or expensive parking lots.

Besides getting to work/school, how will you get to food shops, cultural events, friends' homes, sports facilities, laundromats, restaurants, night clubs?

Staying Safe. Is the home in a safe place? Will you feel safe walking to this apartment at night? There are definitely some communities that will make you feel more comfortable than others. In some neighborhoods, you may feel safer if your building has a concierge or alarm system. In others this may not be necessary. Ask a friend to recommend a good neighborhood.

Cost. You may find that the most convenient places to live are the most expensive. You will have to decide if the convenience and saved time are worth the extra cost.

If You Have Children. Will you be close to good schools? In the US, children in public schools usually go to the school in their neighborhood (although Boston and Cambridge have some exceptions to this rule — see the *If You Have Children* chapter). In general, schools in a school district will be of similar quality. If your child will go to a private school, you may live in any community. But think about how much driving you will have to do to get your child to school, friends' homes, and after-school activities.

Comparing Areas. Try to find two or three areas or communities that you like, so you will have more homes to consider. Be patient and, most of all, be flexible. Do not try to find a home that is exactly like what you left behind in your home country. Most people find some things that they like better here than at home, and other things that they prefer at home.

Working with a Real Estate Agent

We recommend that you work with a real estate agent, whether you want to rent or buy a home. It is possible to find a home without one and, in a few cases, it may be slightly less expensive to do so. For example, if you are renting and do not use an agent, you may avoid paying an agent's fee. However, an agent can:

- discuss individual communities in light of your needs,

Lists of Rentals

Besides real estate agents or university housing offices, you can also find available apartments for rent in these newspapers:

Boston Globe
  realestate.boston.com/
  section/renting/
Boston Herald
  homefind.bostonherald.
  com/

or on many web sites:

boston.craigslist.org
realestate.wickedlocal.com
www.bostonapartments.com
www.rent.com
www.apartments.com
www.bostonforrent.com
www.apartmentguide.com

These sites list apartments to share or to sublet for short periods of time:

boston.craigslist.org/search/
sub
www.sublet.com

Vocabulary for Renting

sublet: rent from another renter, not the owner; some leases prohibit such subletting

landlord: owner of a rental property

studio apartment: one room (combined bedroom and living room) with a small kitchen at one end, plus separate bathroom; also called an efficiency apartment

one- (two- or three-) bedroom apartment: apartment with separate living room, bathroom, kitchen and 1, 2, or 3 bedrooms (a bedroom usually has a window and a closet, regardless of size)

condominium (condo): an apartment that you buy rather than rent

furnished apartment: furniture, dishes, cookware included

heated apartment: cost of heat is included in rent

loft apartment: an apartment, usually with open high-ceiling floor plan; often in converted industrial building or above commercial business

- explain Massachusetts' real estate laws, forms, inspections, choices, deposits, and more,
- help you with your other moving needs, like renting furniture, or understanding public transportation.

There are many rental agents in Boston. Ask a friend or ask at your school if they can recommend one. Find an agent who is willing to work in more than one community, and who is willing to go with you to look at homes. This way, you will have your agent's help and advice.

If you are a student, pick an agent who is used to working with students.

If you are buying a home, it is helpful to have an agent who is a member of at least one Multiple Listing Service (MLS). The MLS gives the agent information about 90% of all homes for sale in the community.

Once you pick an agent, give him or her the chance to get the job done. Do not have two or more agents compete with each other to find you a home. If you decide to change agents, tell the first one about your decision so she or he stops trying to find you a home.

Renting a Home

The Terms
When you find an apartment or home you like, you may be able to negotiate a lower rent or add some requests (for example, new paint, or a new refrigerator). However, usually, you will

be accepting the home *as is* (with no changes). Discuss this with your agent and/or the landlord. You may be asked to put down a deposit to hold the home for you while they get the paperwork started. Ask if the deposit is refundable in case something happens and you do not take the apartment. Write a check for the deposit so you have a receipt.

The Application

Then, when you have settled the offer, you will be asked to complete an application. The application will ask for *credit references*. List your bank and ask the agent how to proceed with the other sections. Often, students will need a cosigner for their lease. Ask the agent if it must be someone in the US. Your school may be able to help you.

The Lease. Some apartments are rented *month-to-month* (either you or your landlord can decide when you will move out by providing 30 days written notice). However, most apartments are *leased*. When you sign a lease, you agree to live in the apartment and pay the rent every month for a certain amount of time, usually twelve months. Because of the number of people in Boston connected to colleges and universities, many Boston rental agreements run from September 1 through August 31.

Although most landlords use a standard lease form, they are allowed to make changes that you should review carefully. An agent can help you. Be sure you understand any *termination penalties* or *buy-out clauses* — if you want to move out before the end of your lease, what will happen? You should also get an *apartment condition statement* that you should review carefully. It will describe the condition of the apartment. Before

Vocabulary for US Homes

powder room or half bath: room with toilet and sink but no shower or bathtub

eat-in kitchen: kitchen with enough room for a table and chairs

breakfast room or alcove: space for informal dining, next to kitchen

living room: main sitting and entertaining space

family room: a less formal living room

den or study: small sitting room in addition to living room

master bedroom: largest bedroom, often with bathroom attached

nursery: small bedroom, for babies or children

pantry: room next to kitchen for storing food and/ or dishes

foyer or front hall: space near front door for greeting people

linen closet: closet with shelves, for towels and bed sheets

walk-in closet: closet that is big enough to walk into

finished basement: basement with covered floors, walls, and ceiling

utility room: room for clothes washer and clothes dryer

patio: outdoor sitting area, usually paved

deck: outdoor sitting area, usually made of wood

porch: outdoor sitting area, usually covered

Real Estate Terms and Abbreviations

LR	living room
BR	bed room
K	kitchen
EIK	eat-in-kitchen
MBR	master bedroom
FR	family room
GAR	garage
WD	clothes washer and dryer
WW	wall-to-wall carpet
DD	dishwasher and disposal
CAC	central air conditioning
FP	fire place
HWF	hard wood floors
ELV	elevator
PKG	parking
HT/HW	heat and hot water

signing this, check to be sure the appliances and plumbing work, and make note of any cracked paint, broken hinges, cracked windows, marks on the walls, etc. At the end of your lease, you may be asked to pay for repairs for any damage or wear not listed in this statement. Be sure you look at it carefully.

Deposits

You may be asked to pay the first and last month's rent, a security deposit (usually equal to one month's rent), and a fee for the agent (also usually equal to one month's rent). In other words, you may need to write a check for $4000 for a $1000/month apartment. You will get the security deposit back (with interest) when you leave if there has been no damage to the home.
The rental market changes from year to year in Boston. You may see special deals, like "half fee" or "no fees" or discounts on rent. Always ask if there are any specials or discounts available, and make sure to get a receipt for the deposit.

Documents

Make a photocopy of all these rental documents (especially things you have signed) and keep them in a safe place.

Maintenance

Maintenance is usually the landlord's responsibility. Do not be shy about calling your landlord if you have a problem with your heat, hot water, plumbing, etc.

Roommates

If you would rather live with roommates than alone, you may be able to find a friend (or some friends) to live with and look for a place together. There are many larger apartments around Boston that are usually rented by groups of students or young professionals. You can often find as many as five bedrooms. Or, you may move into an apartment where the current tenant is looking for a roommate. Universities keep a list of students looking for roommates. Or look in the free newspaper Roommate Magazine in the roommate listings. Or look on-line at a sites like **www.roommates.com, www.roomster.com, www.easyroommate.com** or **boston.metro roommates.com.** Usually for services like these you pay a fee and they will help match you with a roommate.

When you go to see an apartment and interview the current tenant, ask questions like:

- Will you have to sign a lease?
- How much is the rent each month and how much of that is your share? Are utilities included?
- What will happen if your roommates do not pay their rent? Does it become your responsibility?
- Do you need to provide your own furniture?
- Do roommates share groceries? chores?
- Are there are any pets in the apartment?
- Is noise going to be a problem? If you need quiet time to study, say so.
- What are the roommates' attitudes towards smoking, alcohol, and drugs?
- What are roommates' personal habits, like early and late hours and overnight guests?

Expect to be asked the same questions.

Usually with a roommate situation, you will pay less over all. You might be asked for just first and last month's rent or you could be asked to pay a

Insurance for Renters or Homeowners

If you buy a home, you will probably want to buy **homeowners insurance** (and if you use a mortgage to pay for the home, the bank will probably require you to buy it). This insurance will pay for damage to the house that results from such things as fire or floods.
Whether you buy or rent, you may also want:

- **liability insurance** (to protect you if someone sues you), and

- **personal property insurance** (against theft of or damage to your belongings, like television, stereo, silver; be sure to discuss with an insurance agent exactly what you own that will be in your house, because some very expensive items — like art work, jewelry, or computers — may require extra insurance)

Home Buying Help

Try these sites for information about buying a home and sample prices in the Boston area:

realestate.boston.com
www.realtor.com

Row house or *Town house* or
Brownstone (Each floor may
be rented as one or several
separate apartments.)

Victorian (May be split up
into several apartments.)

Duplex or *Two-family* (Any
style of house may be made
into two (or three) apartments, either side by side, or
on separate floors.)

High Rise Building (Many
apartments on each floor,
may have elevator.)

security or utility deposit to your roommate. Write
a check so you have a record of what you paid.

If You Have a Problem with a Landlord

Landlords are required by law to maintain their
apartments and houses in good repair, and to
ensure that you have hot water and heat. If you
have a problem, call the state's Consumer Affairs
Office (**www.mass.gov/ocabr**) or (617) 973-
8787). On their website, click "Contact Us" to
find an on-line Question or Complaint form. They
can help you know whether you can legally stop
paying rent until the problem is fixed, or pay to
have the problem repaired and demand re-pay-
ment. Be sure to get their (or other legal) advice
in such cases.

Buying a Home

If you know you will be in Boston for several
years you may decide to buy a home (house
or condominium) as an investment. Buying a
home often takes several weeks or months, and
includes many legal and financial steps. A real
estate agent can help you through the process.

When you find a home you would like to buy, you
will be asked to fill out an offer form. On the offer
form, you can say:
• when you would like to buy the home,
• how long a mortgage would you like to get
  from a bank,
• what you would like included with the home
  (e.g. refrigerator, lighting fixtures), and
• that you would like the home inspected.
At this time, you will probably be asked to leave a
deposit (money, in the form of a check) with your
offer. Requesting a written offer and deposit is

very common real estate practice, but it is not the law. A real estate agent must tell the seller about any verbal (non-written) offer that you make, no matter how low.

The seller may accept your offer, reject it, or make a *counter-offer* (say no, but make a compromise proposal).

Although a seller is required to tell you about any problems with the home, you should also have the home inspected by a neutral person. Your agent can tell you the names of several qualified inspectors. They will look for such problems as roof leaks, termites, furnace problems, or rotting wood.

Once the offer is accepted by the seller and the house has been inspected, you may be asked to sign a *purchase and sale agreement*. You may want to have a lawyer who specializes in real estate law read this agreement before you sign it. If possible, find a lawyer who has experience working with international buyers, in case there are special visa or banking issues.

Your real estate agent can give you information about getting a *mortgage* (borrowed money to buy your house) if you need to do this. The process can take several weeks or months. You will need to give information about your credit history, salary, and financial status. The bank will usually require you to buy home-owner's insurance. Your agent and lawyer can explain what you need to know to complete your purchase.

Lead Paint

Especially if you have a child under age 6, you will probably hear about the Massachusetts

Cape (Usually covered in wooden shingles, the houses are typically two-stories with 2-3 bedrooms upstairs and a simple lay-out.)

Colonial (Doors, windows and room lay-out are often symmetrical. May be brick or wood, with 3-6 bedrooms upstairs.)

Split Level (Named because the living area is on one level and the family and sleeping areas are on different levels.)

Ranch (Usually all rooms are on one floor. May have a living-dining room in an "L" shape, and typically 3 bedrooms.)

Contemporary (Complex room lay-out varied ceiling heights. Open and sunny.)

Boston Communities

Learn more about communities in the Boston area at:

www.neighborhoodscout.com/ma/boston/

Lead Law when you begin to buy or rent a home. Lead poisoning (which may happen when children eat even small amounts of paint or dust that contains lead) can cause learning and behavior problems. Lead paint was commonly used in houses before 1975, but no longer is permitted. The Lead Law describes the conditions when owners may be required to have lead paint removed from their homes. Ask your real estate agent to explain how or whether this law applies to you.

BOSTON NEIGHBORHOODS AND SURROUNDING AREAS

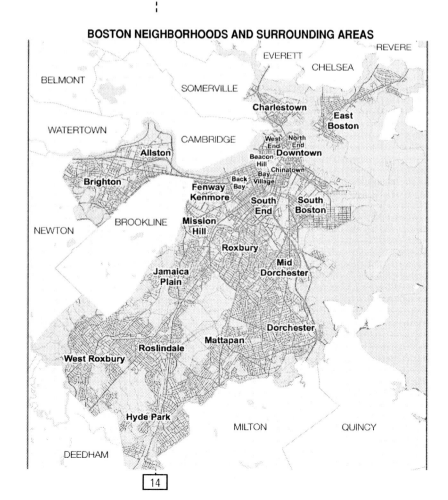

Setting Up
Your Home

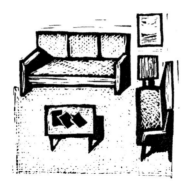

Utilities

Students living in campus housing should ask which utility fees are included in their rent. Usually electricity, gas, oil, telephone service, water, and trash removal are included (and you do not have to set up the account) but long distance telephone service and cable television are not. An internet connection to the school's network for your computer may be included.

If you are renting an apartment, condo, or house, ask your rental agent or landlord which, if any, utilities are included. If you are moving into an apartment with roommates who live there already, ask which, if any, utilities are included in your rent and which you pay for separately.

If you are buying a home, you will need to open your own account with utility companies.

It may take several days to set up utility accounts so it is a good idea to call the companies as soon as you know your new address and move-in date. Each provider is different and will ask you for different information. Be patient when calling the utility companies. It is common to wait on hold for several minutes before a person gets on the line to assist you.

Oil

If you have an oil-burning furnace, you will need to find a reliable oil company. There are many in the Boston area, and most provide similar service. They deliver oil either every two weeks or once a month, depending on how large the oil tank is. They also will service your oil burner and make repairs as necessary. Whether you are renting or buying, we suggest that you check with the owner of your house to see if the current oil company has been giving good service. If they have, stay with them. Call the oil company and notify them of the change of occupant. No deposit is required.

Gas

If you are moving into an apartment with a gas stove or if you are moving into a house and you have a gas stove, gas heat, and/or a gas water heater, you will need gas service. For service in most of Boston, call National Grid (see Sidebar). Except in special circumstances, they can open your account over the telephone. If you do not have a social security number, they may ask you to fax them a copy of your identification.

Most (but not all) neighboring towns and suburbs are served by National Grid or Eversource. Outside of Boston, ask your rental agent or landlord whom to call. You can also try an Internet search using your town name and the word *gas*.

Electricity

If you are moving into a house or apartment, you will need to set up electric service unless electricity is included in your rent. In Boston call Eversource. Except in special circumstances, they can open your account over the telephone. Outside of Boston, ask your rental agent or landlord whom to call. You can also try an Internet search using your town name and the word *electricity*.

Water

Water is generally included in the rental cost of an apartment. If it is not, in Boston the account must be in the property owner's name (not yours). She/he may require you to pay the bill.

Gas and Electricity Companies

National Grid (gas)
(800) 233-5325
www.nationalgridus.com

Eversource (electricity)
(800) 592-2000
www.eversource.com

If you are buying a home, you will need to establish your own account with the town or city Water Department. You must give them your name and address. No deposit is required. The cost of water varies a lot from town to town. Ask your real estate agent about the water rates in towns that interest you.

Trash Removal and Recycling

Boston and most towns arrange for curbside recycling for private homes and most apartments. If you are renting, your landlord will provide for trash removal. She/he may provide a dumpster behind your building or another central area for you to take your trash. Ask your rental agent or landlord about trash.

"The voice on the telephone told me to "enter my account number then press the pound key." I didn't know that the pound key looks like this: #"

For information about recycling drop off centers in Boston call (617) 635-4900. Or go to **www. boston.gov/trash-day-schedule** for detailed information about recycling in the city of Boston.

Outside of Boston, ask your rental agent or landlord about recycling rules. You can also try an Internet search using your town name and the word *recycling*.

Appliances and Electric Plugs

US standard voltage is 110/120 volts, 60 cycles AC. Before using any appliances from your home country, check the voltage ratings marked on them. Many newer appliances and computers have an internal or external switch allowing them to function as a dual voltage item. Look on the back or bottom of the appliance for instructions. You may also need an adapter plug so you can plug the appliance into the US outlet.

Electrical appliances sold in the US come with a cord and 2- or 3-prong plug attached. In some cases (including most new lamps), one of the two prongs is slightly larger than the other. This polarized plug ensures that you put the plug into the outlet in the correct position, so that the current flows in the safest direction. If you have trouble plugging something in, try turning the plug upside down. Some appliances have a third prong on the plug which makes a separate connection to ground and keeps you from getting a shock.

Decorating Your Home

Your new space may not feel like home until you have hung posters, shelves, or lamps. Some dorms and apartments may have rules about what, where or how you hang such things, so be sure to find out about this before you start.

You may learn a lot about American construction methods when you begin this process. Many homes are built with wooden studs (pieces of lumber) spaced 16 inches apart, covered in wallboard. Nails hammered into the wallboard will only support light-weight items. For heavier items, try to find the studs (by tapping along the wall until the sound changes) and put your nails there (through the wallboard and into the wood). If you are unsure how to hang something, cannot use the stud, or are living in a space without wall studs (for example, with brick walls), go to a hardware store and describe your problem. They will help you know what to buy and how to use it.

"I was surprised when I plugged in my fan and found no switch on the wall socket. I didn't realize that I just had to turn the fan on since current starts flowing when you plug in an appliance. At home, we have a 'main switch' next to the socket."

Do It Yourself

If you find that your new home needs minor repairs, you might want to fix them yourself. For some help, go to:

www.doityourself.com (see links on different repairs)

www.hometime.com (the site of a television show about home repair)

www.thespruce.com/home-repair-and-renovating-4127862

www.hometips.com

Connecting
to the World

Telephone Directory

You may, but may not, receive a paper copy of a telephone directory when you set up land line service. If you do not, you can request one (for free) from Dex Media by calling 877-243-8339.

Or, use an online telephone directory:
www.dexpages.com/index.php
Search for an individual (residence) in the White Pages section, or for a business (by name or type) in the Yellow Pages section.

Or click on Find Your Directory on the Map, choose your city, and view the paper director, for Residences, Businesses or Government offices. There, you will also find extensive information about landline services in the Community section.

Some other on-line search options include:
www.superpages.com
www.yellow.com
www.yellowpages.com

Land Line Telephones

If you move into a house or apartment, you may want land line telephone service at your new home, although many people choose not to get home telephone service and use only mobile/ wireless/ cellular service (see page 28 for information on mobile phones and services).

If you do decide to get a land line, there are a number of telephone companies providing local service; the largest is Verizon. To set up service with them, call (800) 837-4966 anytime. Except in special circumstances, you can open your account over the telephone. They may require a deposit.

If you are a student living on campus, your room or suite may have telephone service, but you may need to get a PIN (Personal Identification Number) to call out or to make long distance phone calls.

Choosing Service

If you have a choice in services, here is some useful information. There are four levels of home telephone service: **local** (in and around your city), **regional toll** (outside your local area code but which are not considered long distance), **long distance** (outside the regional calling area but inside the U.S.), and **international** (to other countries). Many local service providers offer all four levels of service although many people choose different providers for their long distance and international calls. You can find telephone service providers by searching for *Telephone Service Providers* on line.

For your local service, you will have several options. If you plan to make very few calls, you can buy a very basic service in which you pay for each call. Most people get an *unlimited local calling* plan that lets them make an unlimited number of local calls for the same monthly fee. If you make a lot of local calls, this might be the best plan for you.

Touch-tone service is the default service for most residential telephone lines but make sure you are receiving this service when you make your telephone plan selection. It costs a little more but you will need it for calls to businesses (especially banks).

For regional toll and long distance service there are a number of choices (see Sidebar for examples). Call them to compare rates and order service. Sometimes they have special rates if you sign up and pay your bill on-line. Check their websites. It usually makes sense to go on one of their special rate plans. You may pay a small monthly fee (which might be waived if you make a certain number of calls or pay on-line), but you will get a better per-minute fee. Some carriers are now offering flat rates with which, for a flat fee per month, you can make an unlimited number of local phone calls.

Most carriers offer international calling plans that give you a discount on calls made outside the US. The details of these plans differ and often change. There is usually a monthly fee. If you call home even a few times a month, paying the fee to get the better rate might save you money.

You do not have to sign up for long distance service. Some people choose not to and use

Toll and Long Distance Telephone Service Providers

All of these telephone numbers offer information in English or Spanish:

- www.att.com
  1(800) 222-0300

- www.comcast.com
  1(800) 266-2278

- www.rcn.com
  1(800) 746-4726

- www.sprint.com
  1(800) 877-4646

- www.verizon.com
  1(800) 837-4966

Optional Special Telephone Services

Call Waiting
If someone is trying to call you when you are talking on the phone, you can put the first caller "on hold" while you talk to the second.

Call Forwarding
Allows you to have your calls automatically ring at a different telephone number whenever you like.

Three-Way Calling
Allows you to add a third person to your call.

Speed Calling
You can program the telephone to automatically dial your most commonly used numbers. (This feature is free on many telephones.)

Caller ID
Displays the name and telephone number of the person calling you (you buy the display panel or telephone with a screen).

Home Voice Mail
A voice mail answering service. You may be able to create different mailboxes for different users.

Repeat Dialing
Re-dials the last number you called. If it is busy, it will try again and signal you when the line is free.

Call Return/*69
Allows you to re-dial the last person who called you.

prepaid phone cards or wireless phones to make long distance phone calls.

When you order your local telephone service, you can add on special features. See the Sidebar for some examples. Each extra service costs extra money each month. Your service provider may bundle some of its most popular features so that you get them as a package cheaper than if you buy them separately. There may be a fee to start features but not to cancel them.

You may be able to bundle your local telephone service with cable television and/or high-speed Internet Access with a provider like AT&T (1-800-222-0300), Verizon (1-800-837-4966), RCN (1-800-746-4726) or Comcast (1-800-266-2278). Bundling (buying several services together) usually saves you money.

Your Telephone
You must buy your own land line telephone(s). You can get one at nearly any hardware store, department store, office supply store, discount appliance store, electronics store, or even drug store. Some telephones have built-in answering machines, speakerphone options, memory options, and/or caller ID screens. The more features you want, the more you will pay. There will be many options ranging from plain corded telephones (about $10) to cordless telephones to high-tech cordless telephones (over $100). At minimum you need a push-button telephone with a "tone" option, not just "pulse".

Directory Listing
Unless you request otherwise, your telephone number will be printed in the White Pages of the telephone book for free and will be available to

anyone who calls Directory Assistance. You can request your number to be "non-directory listed" and it will not be put in the telephone book. If you would like your number not to be in the telephone book *and* not given out by Directory Assistance, then request to be "non-published". Although it may seem unfair, you will pay a fee for these options.

Telephone Bills

Unless you get all levels of services (local, regional toll, long-distance and international) from the same carrier, you may get separate phone bills from each carrier. Long distance and international bills will probably be itemized — every number you called will be listed along with the time, length and cost of the call.

Always check your bill carefully and look for charges that you don't recognize. Sometimes unscrupulous companies "slam" telephone numbers; they switch your account to their service without asking you and charge you high rates. There is also a problem called "cramming," when a company adds charges to your local telephone service for services you did not order. The best way to protect yourself from these practices, which are illegal, is to ask your local service provider to put a "freeze" on your account. That way no one can make changes to your account without your authorization. If you see charges on your bill that you do not understand, call your local service provider for help.

Public Telephones

Public telephones are still available but there are only a few hundred in the entire city of Boston. Read the instructions on the side of the telephone because telephones run by different com-

"I tried to order telephone service on-line. But the on-line form asked me for my current telephone number. I didn't have one of course, so I left it blank. It wouldn't let me continue with this field blank, and I was very frustrated!"

"I was confused when I saw a telephone number that had letters in it. Then I saw the tiny little letters on the telephone pad and realized I should dial using those letters — if the letter is A, B, or C, I should dial a 2, if the letter is D, E, or F, I should dial a 3, etc."

Telephone Numbers

911   An emergency number, to get immediate police, fire, or medical help. See Emergencies Chapter.

611   AT&T Customer service - call if you have questions.

411   AT&T Local and National Directory Assistance. If you cannot find a number in your telephone book, call this number. There may be a fee for this service.

(area code) number   Boston has added new area codes to existing areas. Your neighbor or house-mate may have a different area code than you. You must now dial 10 digits (area code and number), even for local calls. In other parts of the US, you may need to dial only the 7-digit number, without the area code.

(800), (888), (877), (866) or (855)   Toll-free Numbers. When you dial any number with the area code of (800), (888), (877), (866) or (855), you do not have to pay for the call, whether you dial it from home or most pay phones.

(900)   Numbers with the (900) area code are used by companies or individuals for sales, surveys, or for social reasons. The person dialing the number pays a fee — often a fairly large one. For a small one-time fee, you can ask to have these numbers blocked from your service.

1   Dial 1 before the area code and number when calling a long-distance or toll-free number from a land line (but not from a cell phone): 1-617-123-4567.

011   To direct-dial an international call and have it charged to the telephone account you are calling from, dial 011-country code-city code-telephone number.

01   To have an operator help you make an international call, dial 01-country code-city code-telephone number. You can give her your credit card number, reverse the charges, or charge the call to another number.

panies and in different towns have different rules. Local calls (within or near the town from which you are calling) usually cost 35-50¢. At coin telephones, lift the receiver. Put dimes, nickels, or quarters in the coin slot. (Coin telephones do not give change, so have the correct coins ready.) Then enter the telephone number. If the person you are calling is not there, hang up. Your coins will be returned. If the person is there, you may talk for three minutes. After three minutes, an automated voice will interrupt and ask you to put in more money. If you do not add more money, the call will be disconnected. To make long-distance calls from a coin telephone, read the instructions on the front of the telephone. Some public telephones accept only phone cards (bought at stores) or credit cards from your long-distance company.

Phone Cards

Buy a pre-paid phone card at almost any convenience, drug, grocery, or office supply store. The store will activate the card. Or order one on-line by credit card (for example, at www.phonecards. com) and get your PIN numbers through e-mail. Then, at any telephone (private or public), dial the number on the card (usually begins with 1-800). A recorded voice will ask you to enter the PIN or Card number. You can talk for as many minutes as you have left on the card. There are many different types of phone cards, including ones for international calls only. Make sure you read all of the instructions before making a purchase.

Keep in Touch with Your Family

- Join the international calling plan of your long distance telephone service.

- Use a pre-paid telephone card.
  www.phonecards.com
  www.pennytalk.com
  www.idphonecard.com

- Use a 10-10 phone number. This is a way to make an international call without joining any international calling plan or dialing a long series of PIN numbers. Most 10-10 phone numbers are billed to your local phone bill. Go to: www.1010phonerates. com, a website that provides a complete, accurate comparison to help you make an educated choice among different 10-10 phone numbers.

night and weekend minutes: time when lower rates typically apply; usually Monday to Thursday 9 pm to 7 am and Friday 9 pm to Monday 7 am (ask your provider for exact times)

anytime minutes: many plans offer some number of minutes you can use "any time" during the day before being charged

roaming: using a wireless telephone outside your home coverage area; look for global roaming or international roaming service if you want to make or receive calls from other countries

GSM: telephones use SIM cards to identify the owner; some wireless services in the US use a different system, like CDMA or TDMA

rollover minutes: unused minutes from a previous month you can carry over to the next month

data plan: amount of internet access you will be allowed as part of your base fee

Cell (Mobile, Wireless) Telephones

There are many cell phone (also called **mobile phone or wireless telephone**) providers to choose from, including Sprint PCS, AT&T, T-Mobile, MetroPCS, Virgin Mobile and Verizon Wireless. Some, like T-Mobile, specialize in international coverage. You will see cell phones for sale almost everywhere, in electronics stores, at shops and kiosks at the mall, even at convenience stores. Every provider offers different plans at different prices. Here is some information to help you choose:

First, you must choose which service provider and level of service you want. Most wireless telephone plans include caller-ID, voice mail, three-way calling, and call forwarding. Most also have the option of text messaging and wireless internet service over your phone.

Think about how much you plan to use the telephone. Rate plans are based on how many minutes you will use each month, and how often (if at all) you will text or access the internet using your telephone. You pay a certain fee for so many minutes per month, for example, $50 for 500 minutes. If you use 500 minutes or less in a month, your bill will be $50. But there will also be an extra fee (called an "overage"), say 30¢ each minute you go over 500. So if you use 600 minutes in a month your bill would be $50 plus $30 (100 x 30¢) or $80. It usually makes sense to get a plan with more minutes than you need because the overage rates are pretty high.

If you want to text or access the internet using your telephone, you will also need a texting and a data plan, allowing a certain level of access per month (2GB to unlimited, for example). (For reference, 1 MB is roughly equal to 50 emails or viewing 6 web pages or watching 30 seconds on youtube. One GB is roughly equal to sending 50,000 emails, viewing 5,600 web pages or posting 2000 photos to Facebook.) Data plans are sometimes bundled with minute limits, making comparison shopping difficult.

Second, decide which telephone you want. Prices range from several hundred dollars to free from certain providers if you use their service. If you already own a telephone and it uses TDMA or CDMA technology, you may (but may not) be able to use it in the US. Take it to a provider and ask if they can provide service on it; they will need to see the telephone.

Some cell phones in the US use GSM technology. Some GSM telephones are SIM-locked so that you cannot swap out SIM cards. It is possible to buy SIM-unlocked GSM phones in the US but they are often expensive (over $100). If you own a SIM-unlocked multi-band GSM phone that can transmit on the 1900 frequency, you should be able to use it in the US. To save you from paying international rates to make local calls, some wireless providers can provide you with a prepaid US SIM card. It will include a US telephone number, airtime minutes, and other services on your phone without needing to sign a contract. If you are not sure if your phone will be compatible with a US SIM card, take your telephone to a provider and ask.

If you do not have a credit history in the US you may be asked to pay a deposit. You will be asked to sign a term contract that may have early-termination fees. If you do not want to sign

Cell (Mobile, Wireless) Telephone Service

AT&T
www.att.com

MetroPCS
www.metropcs.com

Sprint
www.sprint.com

T-Mobile
www.t-mobile.com

Verizon Wireless
www.verizonwireless.com

Virgin Mobile
www.virginmobile.com

Many of these services provide prepaid cell phone service.

Staying in Touch at Home

Instant messaging

With instant messenger, you can send an instant message to friends who are also on-line. Try these (or check the App Store on your mobile phone):

> hangouts.google.com
> messenger.yahoo.com
> whatsapp.com

Video Calling

Chat, with video, using a service like:

> Apple's Facetime
> Microsoft's Skype
> Google's Hangout
> Facebook's Messenger
> www.icq.com

Staying in touch

Social networking sites make it much easier for you to stay in touch with family and friends at home. Check out the following sites or search on-line for other social networking sites.

> www.facebook.com
> www.twitter.com
> www.instagram.com
> www.snapchat.com

Blogs

Describe your experience in a blog, with photographs. descriptions of your daily life, things that surprise you, and your new friends.

> www.wordpress.com
> www.blogger.com
> www.tumblr.com

a contract or pay a deposit, you can ask about prepaid plans. With these plans you buy the telephone, pay an activation fee, and buy minutes to use in advance. When your prepaid minutes are used up, you can buy more. Most providers have a prepaid option.

Cell Phone Etiquette

It is generally expected that you will turn your cell phone off during classes, at lectures, in libraries, and at concerts and movies. Other places, including some restaurants, have a no-cell-phone policy. If you are expecting a really important call, turn the ringer off and set it to vibrate or flash when you get a call instead.

Internet Access

Students living on campus may have a connection to their school's network in their room or suite. Even if they live off campus, their school may have a way to access its network. If it does, you may not need an Internet Service Provider.

Most people choose to have a high-speed internet connection but dial-up service is still available. (Fewer than 3% Americans use dial-up service.) To use a dial-up service, your computer will need a modem and you may need special software that will be provided when you sign up. Dial-up uses your telephone line, so you cannot make or receive phone calls when you are on-line.

High-speed Internet connections like DSL or cable modem service are now available in most Boston neighborhoods. DSL works over your telephone line but you can still make and receive calls when you are on-line. Cable modems provide service over your cable line instead of your telephone line. Service called Broadband can refer to either DSL or Cable. You generally need a special modem to use DSL or a cable modem and you may need to pay a technician to install it.

Some Internet Service Providers offer month to month service. Others require you to sign a contract for a year or more. Many providers offer promotional deals to encourage you to sign up with them. Always ask if they have such an offer. Ask if they will match their competitors' offers, too. Some neighborhoods and apartment buildings have a specific service provider you will have to use if you want broadband service. The availability of promotional deals may also be limited by your location.

Smart phones with data plans provide internet access. Some individuals find that this access is all that they need. For you this will depend on your habits and your smart phone capabilities.

Wireless Fidelity (Wi-Fi)
If you have a notebook computer that is Wi-Fi enabled, you can receive a wireless signal in Wi-Fi hot spots, public places that provide Wi-Fi Service. Hot spots have grown more common in the US in the past few years. Coffee houses, bookstores, hotels and other sites often provide free Wi-Fi for customers. You may need a password or agree to 'terms of service' before the connection works. To find a Wi-Fi zone near you, visit **www.wififreespot.com/mass.php.** To use public Wi-Fi, hot spot operators may expect you to manually configure your Wi-Fi cards with little or no technical support. So you do not have

Internet Service Providers
www.aol.com
www.earthlink.net
www.comcast.com
www.netzero.net
www.rcn.com
www.verizon.com

Wicked Free Wi-Fi
The City of Boston has a free wi-fi system accessible in over 130 outdoor access points - "Wicked Free WiFi.". Plans are to expand the availability to other parts of the city in the next several years. A map of the current wi-fi availability can be found at:

www.cityofboston.gov/doit/wifi/

Internet Telephone Service (VoIP)

Comcast
www.comcast.com

Vonage
www.vonage.com

Skype
www.skype.com
Free computer-to-computer
phone calls.

to reconfigure each time you use a hot spot, some ISPs offer special Wi-Fi plans that will let you use public Wi-Fi signals automatically.

Email

In addition to providing you with Internet access, most ISPs will provide you with an email account. Students probably also get a free email account through their university or college. Or, there are many free, web-based email services like gmail, icloud.com and Yahoo! Mail. You can access your email account from any computer or cell phone with Internet access. Some also offer spam/junk email filters and free virus screening for email attachments.

Internet Telephone Service

Internet telephone service (also called Voice over IP or VoIP) provides telephone service over the internet. In some cases this is provided through your regular internet access provider. This service closely resembles traditional telephone service but is generally less expensive. If you are interested, check with your internet access provider at the time you request service to see if this is something they offer or look on-line to see what may be available in your area. There are many providers of VoIP services. This can be an effective replacement for traditional telephone service. However, VoIP service may not handle emergency (911) calls. Ask your VoIP provider if you will be able to make such calls using its service.

A popular free form of VoIP works from computer to computer using the computer's microphone and speakers to conduct the phone conversation. (See sidebar). Both parties must be enrolled for this to be free. You may be able to purchase additional services at a very low cost from the software developer. Computer-to-computer VoIP is probably most useful as a cost-effective supplement to more traditional land line or wireless telephone services.

Television and Radio

Broadcast Television

To watch broadcast television, you do not need to have a license or to pay a fee. Simply buy a TV and plug it in. You will probably be able to watch several commercial and/or public TV stations this way, although the picture quality may be poor. Public TV stations do not show commercials. Their programming tends to be educational and cultural in nature. Televisions made before 2008 may need a converter box. The Federal Communications Commission has an informative website at **www.fcc.gov/general/digital-television** to answer your questions about digital converters. Digital converters are not required for cable or satellite television.

Cable Television

You may want to order cable television because:
- the reception of local broadcast stations may be much better with cable,
- even with a basic cable TV service, you get a large number of stations, and
- there may be particular stations or services you want that are only available through cable TV (like recent movies, sports or some shows for children).

Broadcast TV and Radio Stations

Commercial Television

WBZ (channel 4)[1]	CBS[2]
WCVB (channel 5)	ABC
WHDH (channel 7)	Ind
WFXT (channel 25)	Fox
WUNI (channel 27)	UNI
WSBK (channel 38)	MNT
WLVI (channel 56)	CW

Public Television

WGBH (channel 2)	PBS
WGBX (channel 44)	PBS

1 local station
2 broadcast company

College and Public Radio

WBUR (90.9) Boston University
WERS (88.9) Emerson
WGBH (89.7), PBS
WHRB (95.3), Harvard
WMBR (88.1), MIT
WUMB (91.9), UMass Boston
WZBC (90.3), Boston College

Satellite TV Services

DirecTV
www.directv.com

Dish Network
www.dish.com

Satellite Radio Services

Sirius XM Satellite Radio
www.siriusxm.com

Cable is a de-regulated industry. Look on line for companies in your community. The largest are Comcast: (888) 266-2278, RCN: (800) 746-4726, and Verizon: (800) 837-4966. Call them or visit their websites to set up your service.

You may want to rent a cable box for an additional fee, even if your television is "cable ready" because it will allow you to receive more stations. Without a cable box you cannot receive premium movie channels (HBO, Showtime, The Movie Channel, etc) or pay-per-view channels. You may also be able to "bundle" other services, such as your internet service and phone, with your cable service. Ask the company what services they provide.

Internet or "Streaming" TV

You can also access many TV shows directly through the internet. Check out amazon.com, hulu.com, netflix.com, itunes.com or vudu.com for more information.

Satellite Television or Radio

Some people choose a satellite service like DirecTV or XM Radio for their TV and radio stations. Generally you need to purchase the equipment and sign a long-term contract. For more information, see the Sidebar or look online.

Radio

You do not need a license or to pay a fee to use a radio. Choose either the AM or FM setting on your radio. You will be able to find music of many types, weather forecasts, sports, news, and talk shows (in which listeners call the announcer to ask questions or give opinions). Most stations are commercial, and carry advertisements. Boston has several college-supported and public radio FM stations that are non-commercial. These tend to have a mix of folk and classical music, jazz, and news.

Internet Radio and Live Stream Music

Many radio stations are also available on the internet. Check to see if your favorite station is available on line. Some will stream a particular type of music (like classical or jazz) all day. Or do an internet search for "streamed radio" then search for the type of music or show you like best.

At Pandora (**www.pandora.com**) you can create your own "station" that plays just the kind of music you are in the mood to hear, by musical style. Or try **www.musicovery.com**, where you select a style of music, an era (like "the 60s" or "the 1940s"), and your mood (for example, calm or energetic), and it plays music that fits the style. Try **www.spotify.com** to create your own playlist and listen to top hits, too. Other options are **www.siriusxm.com, www.iheart.com,** and **www.tunein.com.**

Podcasts

Podcasts allow you to download or subscribe to content on the internet on subjects that are interesting to you. You listen to the podcast at a time that it convenient for you. A podcast can be played on a computer or on a mobile device. When you find information on the web that you particularly like or want to listen to regularly, check the website to see if a podcast from the site is available.

Notes

Money Matters

Money Orders

Money orders are a safe and convenient way to send someone money without relying on checks or credit cards. You can buy and send one at any Post Office. Or many convenience and grocery stores provide Western Union service that allows you to send or receive a money order.

Currency and Checks

Currency

The basis of US currency is the dollar ($), consisting of 100 cents (¢). Coins come in the following values: 1¢ (penny), 5¢ (nickel), 10¢ (dime), 25¢ (quarter), and $1 (buck or dollar). It is important to learn the nicknames, as they are used often in conversation. You may also see a 50¢ coin, but these are rare. The gold-colored dollar coins are relatively new and not very popular, perhaps because they look very similar to a quarter; if you get one, be careful not to spend it as a quarter. Paper bills are all the same size, although the pictures differ on notes of differing value. The new $5, $10, $20, $50 and $100 notes have improved security features, including some background colors and embedded images. Be sure to read the numbers carefully! Notes come in these values: $1, $5, $10, $20, $50, and $100.

Checks

Writing personal checks may be new for you. In the US, you may pay your bills (utility bills, rent, credit card bills) by personal check. You can also often buy things in stores and pay for restaurants by check (as long as you have a credit card and/or picture identification with you, too). Although on-line bill paying and credit card payment are becoming more popular, you may need to use checks occasionally.

Remember to write down the amount of every check you write, and subtract it from the amount of money you have in your account. Your checkbook will have a place to keep this record. The exact amount of money you have may be difficult to track because of service fees being subtracted and/or interest being added.

Watch carefully, though, because if you write a check for an amount you do not have (called an "overdraft" or a "bounced check"), you will have to pay a penalty fee. This is true even if you have plenty of money in another type of account in the same bank. Some banks offer reserve credit (or overdraft protection) — they will cover the amount of the bounced check and charge you interest for this "loan." However, it is often difficult to get this protection if you do not have income or a credit history in this country.

Checks that you receive must be deposited at your bank. You can do this at an ATM or inside the bank with a teller. Some businesses advertise "check-cashing" services. You will receive cash immediately for your check using this service. However, this is not free. You will be charged a fee or a percent of your check. Cashing your check at the bank where you have your account is free.

"In my country, if you use your ATM card to get cash from another bank's ATM, it costs about twenty cents. But here it costs a dollar or two."

Your Name
Your Address
Your City, State Zip Code

5-39/110

1001

DATE *August 1, 2018*

PAY TO THE ORDER OF *City Electric Company* $ *240.33*

Two hundred forty and 33/100 _____ DOLLARS

YOUR BANK NAME

Account #123-45-678   *Your legal signature*

MEMO

00112378945 023 0181934 1001

How to write a personal check

Write the amount both in numbers and in words. Draw a line after the words to fill the space, so no one can change your writing. (In this example, the "bank routing number" is pre-printed in the bottom left-hand corner (0011223344). Your bank "account number" is next (1234567). The last few digits (1001) refer to this specific check.)

- **Proof of who you are:** You will need some form of official identification that includes your photograph, like a passport, driver's license or state ID card.

- **Social Security number:** Bring your Social Security number, for tax purposes, if you have one. Or, if you will not have a Social Security number, the bank will have you complete another (W-8) form.

- **Local mailing address:** Be sure you know all address details (street number and name, apartment number, town, zip code). Bring proof that this is your address, like a signed lease or a letter you have received there.

- **Money to deposit:** Banks require different amounts of money to open an account. You will need to have US dollars or travelers checks.

- **Your mother's maiden name:** The bank will ask you for your mother's maiden name (your mother's family name before she was married) or some other family name. This name is used as a security check when you need to contact the bank with questions.

Bank Accounts

Choosing a Bank

There are many banks to choose from in Boston. Compare them on these features:

Fees and Service Charges. Interest rates, services, and fees vary from bank to bank. A bank may charge a fee you do not expect. Your bank is responsible for letting you know when these fees change in price. Ask about these:

- monthly charges and ways to avoid them
- whether you must maintain a minimum balance
- cost for checks printed with your name and address on them
- cost for each transaction, including processing checks
- cost for using the Automatic Teller Machines (ATMs) at other banks

Interest Rates. Some types of bank accounts pay interest, some do not. Compare the different types and rates of interest-paying accounts at each bank.

Convenience. Is there a branch of the bank or an ATM near your home? Your school? Are the hours convenient for you? How many ATMs does this bank have in your community? Can you do any banking by telephone or computer?

Opening a Bank Account

Most banks offer several kinds of accounts; you can choose more than one:

Checking Account. You need a checking account in order to write checks. You will get a few checks when you open the account. Others, with your name and address printed on them, will be mailed to you. Many stores will not accept checks without this information printed on the check. Money in a checking account may earn no or little interest and there may be a monthly fee to have a checking account. However, some banks offer interest or a no-fee account if you keep a minimum balance in the account. Many large banks also offer checking accounts specifically for students. These accounts usually have fewer fees and penalties.

Savings Account. Money in savings accounts earns some interest. It is common to open both a checking and a savings account. Usually, you can switch money between the two accounts at an automatic teller machine or on-line. This way, you can keep some money in the checking account to cover checks you write, and the rest in an interest-earning savings account. The bank will not make this transfer for you though; you have to do it yourself.

Money Market Account. Money market accounts usually earn more interest than a savings account, but you may be required to keep a minimum balance of several thousand dollars.

Debit/ATM Cards

Order a debit card that is also an ATM card. You can use this card to pay in many stores. Money is taken directly out of your checking account. This can be more convenient than writing a check and is a good alternative to carrying large sums of money in your wallet. Or use it to get cash, look at your balance at any of your bank's ATMs, transfer funds between accounts and, at some machines, buy postage stamps. You will find ATMs in shopping malls, supermar-

Bank Cards

ATM Cards vs. Debit Cards

With an ATM card, you will only be able to withdraw or deposit money into your account at an ATM. You will not be able to buy things with it. With a debit card, you can withdraw or deposit money and use it to buy things in stores, pay for restaurants, or make Internet or telephone purchases. When you use a debit card, the money is automatically withdrawn from your account. You will be given a choice when you set up your account if you wish to have an ATM card or a debit card, or both.

Debit Cards vs. Credit Cards

When you use a debit card, money is withdrawn directly from your checking account. With a credit card, the credit card company pays for the purchase and sends you a bill. You have several weeks to pay them back, and may not have to pay the total amount (but you pay a fee for this lending service).

5 Tips for Getting a Credit Card

1 - If possible, apply for a credit card from a US bank before you actually move here. Even for US residents, there is usually a delay.

2 - Credit unions may be more likely to give you a credit card than a bank. If you are a member of a credit union, try there.

3 - Some (but not all) banks will give you a secured card. You put money into an account. Then you can use the secured credit card to "charge" against that account. You cannot charge more than the amount you have deposited. You will still have the convenience of being able to charge rather than pay by check or cash. And you will be starting a credit history.

4 - If you are employed in the US, ask your employer to write a letter, stating your salary, job position, and (especially if you plan to be here for several years) your length of stay. Try applying for a card at the bank that your employer uses.

5 - If you are offered a card, but with a low credit limit (like $500), accept it and use it. When the bank sees that you pay your bills on time, they will probably increase the credit limit.

kets, airports, and along the street. In addition, there are several networks of banks (like Cirrus, NYCE, and PLUS). For a small fee, you can get cash from an ATM from any bank in your bank's network anywhere in the US and, in some cases, internationally. Sometimes the bank will offer no fee on a certain number of withdrawals each month, check with your bank for their policy.

You will need to choose a secret Personal Identification Number (PIN). You will use this PIN when you use the ATM or debit card. Memorize the PIN and never write it on the card — it is a way to make sure no one uses the card except you. Banks differ in how long the number should be.

Credit Cards

You will find it useful to have a major credit card while living in the US. You can use a credit card in most department stores, gasoline stations, supermarkets, restaurants, and shops. You can use it to make telephone reservations for theaters, concerts, air travel reservations, and car rentals. Even if you do not like to pay with a credit card, it is useful to have one when you pay by check, as a form of identification, and to show that you have passed some bank's credit review. With some credit cards, you can earn frequent flier miles or make donations to organizations you care about (like schools or charities).

You may be able to use a credit card from your bank in your home country. But if you do, each month's bill will go to that bank, and will be charged in that currency. You will be paying for the conversion.

Unfortunately, it is sometimes difficult for international newcomers (students and employed people, alike) in the US to get a credit card from a US bank immediately. Many banks are slow to give credit cards to people who do not have established credit histories in the US (a history of paying debts on time). See the Sidebar for some tips on how to get a credit card.

On-Line Banking

Most major banks offer free on-line bill payment. To see if a bank offers this service, call their Customer Service line or check the bank's web-page. Once you have signed up for access to your account through the web you can pay your bills on-line. The large companies in the Boston area may already be in the bank's database. If not, you can always add the information about the person or company you wish to pay manually. Any person and any company can be paid through on-line banking.

Additional services may be available from your on-line bank account, Check your bank's website to see if it offers these services:
- receiving your bills electronically with email notification directly to you
- automatic payment of specified bills for a regular amount
- ability to se up payment of a bill many days or weeks in advance
- deposit checks remotely via a mobile device

Automatic payments leave you one less thing to worry about. However, if you do not have enough money in your account when the payment is made, you will be charged a big fee.

If you are not certain that you will have enough money in your account at the time the automatic

"I was scared when I went to open a bank account. I was brought into a room. A manager talked to me and asked a lot of questions. Opening a bank account took me half an hour — I thought it would be an easy job and take 10 minutes."

Picking a Password

As you set up your new life in the US, you will probably have to establish many accounts and passwords. Plan ahead to have safe passwords that you can remember. Here are some tips:

Have at least two passwords you use regularly - one for confidential, financial, or legal accounts, the other for everything else. (Many safety experts recommend even more than two.)

Different companies require different lengths and characters for their passwords. Start now with one that is at least 8 characters and includes at least one number, letter and symbol. This will work for nearly all accounts; capitalize some letters for added security.

Don't use a word someone who knows you could guess - your child's name, your pet's name, your anniversary date. Some alternatives:

• Think of a sentence then use the first letter of each word: "We have 3 friends and 2 cousins in Boston" becomes Wh3fa2ciB.

• Replace letters in a word with a similar-looking number or symbol: ! for i, @ for a, $ for S, ^ for v, 3 for E, 5 for S, etc.

payment would be made, it is best to pay the bills manually.

Other On-Line Activities. Even if you do not want to pay your bills electronically, banks' websites can be valuable for other reasons. When you create a login and password name, you can find information about your account, such as current account summaries, past summaries of transactions, payment information, how to change personal information (address, phone number), and how to change account options (for example, to receive e-mail reminders to pay your bill).

Wire Transfers

International wire transfers are one good option for receiving money into your account from another country. Different banks charge different fees, ranging from about $10-$16. Wiring money from the US to another country may be more expensive than receiving it here.

To send an international wire transfer to your US bank, the sender will need your US bank's address, your account number, and your bank's S.W.I.F.T. address and its CHIPS Participant number. (Just ask your bank — they will know what you mean.)

Money Transfers to Friends

You may want to give money to a friend - say, to share a restaurant bill. Some banks have a way to "Send" money to a friend just by knowing their email address. Or try PayPal, Venmo or Google Pay on your smart phone.

Traveling
Around Town

Boston Without a Car

Walking

Often, especially in downtown Boston where there are many narrow, one-way streets and lots of cars, the fastest way to get around town is to walk. Walk on the right-hand side of the sidewalk. If you come from a country where cars drive on the left side of the road, be especially careful to look both ways (first, to the left!) before stepping into the street.

It is safest to cross the street where there is a light and a "Walk" sign. In many parts of Boston,

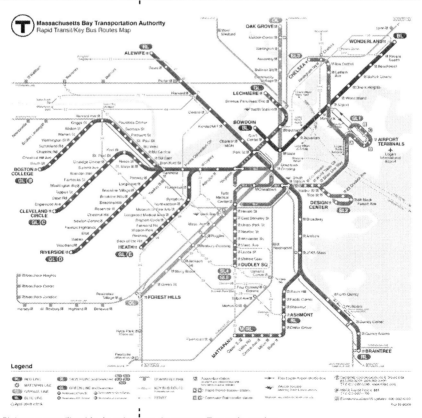

Pick up a map like this, in color, at a downtown T or train station.

there are now crossing areas marked by white stripes painted on the street, and orange markers. The law says that cars and bikes must stop if someone steps off the curb into one of these crossing areas. However, you should always be careful crossing the street, even in the crossing areas.

Biking

Biking is becoming an increasingly popular way to navigate Boston. If you don't have your own bicycle, you may choose to rent a bike for an hour or two. Hubway (**www.thehubway.com**) is a new kiosk-based bike rental system with more than 180 stations and 1800 bikes (and plans for 3000 by end of 2019), in Boston, Cambridge, Brookline and Somerville. Pick up a bike at any kiosk (some have helmets, too) and return it to any kiosk in the system. Hourly, monthly and annual memberships are available.

You can combine bike riding with using mass transit (**www.mbta.com/riding_the_t/bikes**). Additional information is available at **ridethecity.com/boston:** an interactive map with bike shops, rentals, bike shares and suggested routes.

Massachusetts has a bike helmet law. Anyone age 16 and under must wear a helmet when riding a bike or traveling on one as a passenger. Those over age 16 are also advised to wear one as a good safety practice.

Boston has made many improvements for bikers (dedicated bike lanes, easy rentals) but Boston drivers are still not very accustomed to watching for bikes. Be careful. Find additional information about biking in Boston at **www.cityofboston.gov/bikes**.

AAA for Bicycles

The American Automobile Association (see signup information in sidebar on page 54) is now offering roadside assistance for bicycles.

AAA will transport the rider and bicycle anywhere within 10 miles at no cost. A mileage fee will be assessed for transportation beyond 10 miles.

Regular road service guidelines apply to all bicycle calls. Members must be present at the time of service and have a valid AAA card.

See additional information at www.aaa.com.

Who is Charlie?

A political song, *Charlie on the MTA*, written in 1948 to protest a fare increase, became a big hit and is still sung today. In those days, people had to pay a fare to enter a train and another when they exited. In the song, Charlie did not have enough money to get off the train, and so had to "ride forever 'neath the streets of Boston."

MBTA alerts

Sign up at MBTA.com to receive notifications directly from the MBTA of delays and disruptions, as well as advanced notice of planned service changes, by email or text message (SMS). MBTA. com also has additional resources listed for web browsers which can bring many of the capabilities of smartphone apps to your desktop computers.

MBTA - Massachusetts Bay Transit Authority

The MBTA runs subway, bus, commuter rail and boat services for local transportation in the Boston area. **www.mbta.com.**

Interested in knowing when the next bus, train, ferry or T is coming? Check out your smartphone app options at **www.mbta.com/mbta-endorsed-apps**.

Subway. The subway (sometimes called the **T** or the **trolley**) runs both underground (in and close to the city of Boston) and above ground. There are four main lines: Red, Blue, Green, and Orange. (The Silver Line is actually a bus that goes from Downtown Crossing to Dudley Square, and also from South Station to the waterfront and Logan Airport. T passes cover Silver Line fares.) Transfers from one line to another are free at Park Street, Downtown Crossing, State, North Station, and Haymarket.

Hours of operation vary by station and line but are approximately:
> 5:00 am to 12:50 am Monday-Saturday
> 6:00 am to 12:50 am Sunday

Maps showing the train routes are posted at each stop or station, or you can get one at many downtown T stations, or at **www.mbta.com**.

Most rides cost $2.75 ($1.10 for seniors, people with disabilities, and junior or senior high school students; children 11 and younger ride free). If you pay cash, you will need exact change. Or, consider buying a CharlieCard or Charlie-Ticket at one of 100 retail stores, at vending machines in many T stations, or by telephone: (617) 222-3200, or on-line at **www.mbta.com**.

CharlieCards and Tickets store value (like $20) for single or multiple rides (to be deducted with each ride) or for a monthly T-pass (which allows unlimited travel — see below). Rides paid with a CharlieCard are cheaper ($2.25). Tap the Card (or insert a Ticket) on the reader at the station, on the train or bus. If you have stored single or multiple rides, the fare will be deducted from the card.

If you plan to ride the bus or subway regularly, consider purchasing a T pass. There are several types of passes. Your choice will depend on how frequently you will travel, where you will travel, the type of transportation (bus, T, rail) and how far you will travel. The Monthly LinkPass ($84.50/month; $30/month for seniors, people with disabilities and students), the Week Link Pass ($21.25/week), and the Day LinkPass ($12/day) provide unlimited rides on the subway and buses for a month, week, and day, respectively. Monthly LinkPasses should be renewed before the first of each month to avoid long lines.

The MBTA allows animals to ride its trains. Service animals are allowed on the T at all times. During off-peak hours, non-service dogs are allowed at the discretion of the driver. During rush hour, small pets may be carried on the T in lap-sized containers if they are kept away from the exit doors.

Buses. Most buses run from 5:15 am to 12:30 am Monday to Saturday, 6:00 am to 12:30 am Sundays. Select buses run until 2:30 am on Friday and Saturday nights. Go to **www.mbta. com** for schedules. Most local rides cost $2.00, or $1.70 if paid with a CharlieCard. More details in the sidebar on this page. You can also buy

MBTA

The Massachusetts Bay Transit Authority (MBTA) runs the "T," the city buses, and the commuter rail. For information on schedules, maps, passes, and fares, call (617) 222-3200 (Mon.-Fri., 6:30 a.m. to 8:00 p.m.; Sat., Sun., 7:30 a.m. to 6:00 p.m.) or visit www.mbta.com.

MBTA Fares
Trolley/Subway/T:
Charlie Ticket or cash on board: $2.75

Charlie Card: $2.25

Seniors, people with disabilities and students: $1.10

Children age 11 and under ride free.

Buses:
Charlie Ticket or cash on board: $2.00, local rides

Inner suburbs: $5.00
Outer suburbs: $7.00

Charlie Card: $1.70

Seniors, people with disabilities and students: $0.85

Children age 11 and under ride free.

Commuter Rail:
Varies from $2.25-12.50; call (617) 222-3200 or go to www.mbta.com for details

NOTE: MBTA has no immediate plans for increases fares.

Taxi Fares

In Boston, taxis use a meter on the dashboard to show the fare. The fare depends both on how far you go and how long it takes. If you cross a toll bridge or tunnel (like the Callahan Tunnel), the driver will pay the toll then add that amount onto the meter fare.

Meter rates:
$2.60 for the first 1/7 mile or less, then $0.40 for each additional 1/7 mile

Waiting time:
$28 per hour

All trips to Logan Airport
$2.75 surcharge

Station wagon and van taxicabs may charge a $5 fee if a passenger has a lot of luggage, boxes or large items.

See bpdnews.com/taxi-rates for more information from the Boston Police Department.

To estimate the cost of a taxi ride, try:
boston.taxiwiz.com
www.numbeo.com/taxi-fare/in/Boston

a monthly pass that allows unlimited travel on buses for $55 or a Monthly LinkPass that allows travel on both bus and T (see above). To learn which bus route you need or to buy tickets by telephone, call 617-222-3200. Or go to one of the 100 retail stores that sell them, or **www.mbta. com**.

Commuter Rail. The commuter rail line connects suburban towns to Boston (North or South Stations) and/or the ends of trolley routes. Most commuter rail stations have parking lots. Trains run from about 5:30 am to 12:00 midnight, Mondays to Fridays; service on weekends is limited. Trains run about every 30 minutes during rush hour, and every 1-2 hours midday and evening. Commuter rail trains cost from $2.25 to $12.50, depending on the distance and the hour. If you buy your ticket on the train at a station that conveniently sells tickets, you will be charged extra; a $3 surcharge. Have a smart phone? *mTicket* is an app which allows you to purchase tickets. Ten-ride passes (valid for 90 days) and monthly passes are also available. Call (617) 222-3200 or go to **www.mbta.com** for information about the commuter rail fares and schedules.

Taxis

In some countries, taxi drivers must have a lot of experience driving in the city before they can be licensed. They usually know a lot about the city, and keep their taxis clean and in good repair. Boston cab drivers have improved in these areas recently but they may still not compare to your home country taxis. Although many will have GPS to guide them to your destination, if possible, be prepared to give the driver directions.

Despite this warning, you should also know that

taxis are considered quite safe from crime or cheating. It is very rare to hear of a taxi driver hurting or stealing from a passenger.

To get a taxi, you can:

- call a taxi company in the town where you want to be picked up (check the Appendix at the back of this book for a partial listing of taxi companies or look online)

- walk to a taxi stand (often near hotels or train and T stops)

- hail a taxi by waving your hand (some taxis have a light on the roof that shows they are available, but most do not. You can still try to hail a taxi, but it is frustrating because you cannot tell, from a distance, if it is available.)

In some towns, taxis are not allowed to pick up hailing passengers except in the town in which they are registered. For example, a Cambridge-based taxi may take someone to Brookline. Then, while driving back to Cambridge (but while still in Brookline), the driver may see someone trying to hail him or her. The driver is not allowed to pick up that passenger. In this case, the passenger should look for an available taxi from that town, telephone a taxi company, or walk to a taxi stand.

Be sure the taxi you hail is a licensed taxi. Find the name of the taxi company on the side or on top of the car, and the driver's operating license hanging in plain view inside the car. These are both signs that this is a licensed taxi.

Usually, you can call a taxi just 10-15 minutes before you want it to arrive. But sometimes you should call ahead (like holiday times, in rainy or snowy weather, early in the morning, or in the middle of the night). If you are not sure what to

Some Taxi Customs

- Most people pay a taxi driver a 15-20% tip.

- Taxis are not allowed to take more than four passengers. Do not ask a driver to break this rule, as his insurance will be invalid if he does.

- Ride in the back seat of a taxi unless there are four of you. In a group of four, the taxi driver may allow one person to ride in the front seat.

- Feel free to ask a door-man or the driver for an estimate of the cost of the ride before getting in a taxi.

Ride Share Companies

Order a private driver with a smartphone app. Fares are generally lower than taxis and tipping is not necessary:
www.uber.com
www.lyft.com
fasten.com

Sample Fares (uberX)
Base fare: $2.10, then $1.35 for each mile and $0.21 for each minute of trip. Prices may be higher at peak-usage times.
Minimum fare: $6.85
Cancellation fee: $5.00

Larger and more comfort-able vehicles are available at an additional cost. Or use uberPool for a discount.

Written Driver's Test

The written test for a driver's license is available in the following languages:

- Albanian
- Arabic
- Armenian
- Cambodian
- Chinese
- Czechoslovakian
- Farsi (Iranian)
- Finnish
- French
- German
- Greek
- Hebrew
- Hungarian
- Italian
- Japanese
- Korean
- Laotian
- Polish
- Portuguese
- Romanian
- Russian
- Spanish
- Turkish
- Vietnamese

do, call the taxi company and ask whether you should order ahead. Be prepared to give your address and apartment number, first name, and telephone number. The driver may not come to your door, but call or honk the horn instead.
For a complete information about fares, rules, and a list of six local taxi associations, see the City of Boston's official site: **www.bpdnews. com/hackney-carriage-unit**

An alternative to taxi companies is now popular in Boston: **ride-share companies** like Uber, Lyft and Fasten (see sidebar on page 51). Use your smartphone to call a driver. You will see the cost before you confirm your pickup. The driver will appear within a few minutes. No tipping is necessary. Pay with a credit card from your account.

Boston With a Car

Driving practices differ in different parts of the US. It is important to understand Boston driving patterns, so you can avoid an accident. Many Americans from other parts of the US think Boston drivers are rude and aggressive. Of course you should not "go native" and drive this way yourself! But it is important to drive defensively — you should always assume that another car might turn right from the left-hand lane, or that a bike might go through a red light, or a pedestrian walk out in front of you.

Many international newcomers choose to take a one- or two-hour driving lesson with a professional driver education company when they first arrive. This might be an excellent idea for you, especially if you come from a country with very

To Get a Class D Massachusetts Driver's License

1. Get and study a Driver's Manual, in preparation for taking a written test: **www.mass.gov/files/documents/2018/03/26/Drivers_Manual.pdf**.

2. Go to one of the following full-service Registry of Motor Vehicle (RMV) offices. Learn more about each site at **www.mass.gov/orgs/massachusetts-registry-of-motor-vehicles/locations** (hours, services, current wait times).

Boston – 136 Blackstone Street
Braintree - 10 Plain Street
Brockton – 490 Forest Avenue
Fall River – 1794 North Maine Street
Haverhill – 4 Summer Street (City Hall)
Lawrence – 73 Winthrop Avenue, Plaza 114
Leominster– 500 Research Drive
Lowell – 77 Middlesex Street
Milford – 14 Beach Street

New Bedford – 212 TH Rice Boulevard
Plymouth – 40 Industrial Park Road
Revere --- 9c Everett Street
Roslindale – 4210 Washington Street
Taunton – 1 Washington Street
Watertown – 550 Arsenal Street
Wilmington - 355 Middlesex Avenue
Worcester – 611 Main Street

You do not need an appointment. The suburban offices are often less crowded than the Boston office. Bring these with you (and read www.mass.gov/passenger-class-d-drivers-licenses before you go):

- three original (not photocopied) forms of identification that show your date of birth, your signature, and proof of Massachusetts residency. (We suggest your passport, your international or translated home-country driver's license, and a lease, mortgage statement, or utility bill that is no more than 60 days old.)

- proof of your "lawful presence" in the US (immigration documents that show you have legal status to be in the US for at least 12 months) (a new regulation since March 2018)

- your Social Security number or an official letter from the Social Security Administration saying you are not eligible for one, and

- $30 (personal check made payable to MassDOT, money order or credit card)

Complete an application for a "learner's permit." Pass a vision exam. Have your photograph taken. Pass a 25-question written test, available in 24 languages (see Sidebar for a list of the languages). You must answer at least 18 questions correctly. All of the questions come from the Drivers' Manual.

3. Schedule a road skills test by calling (857) 368-8000 or at www.massrmv.com. Note: not all the offices listed above offer the road skills test. At the time of the road skills test, pay $35. You will use your own car. You must come to the appointment with a qualified sponsor unless you are from one of the countries listed in the Convention on Road Traffic of 1949.

4. Pay an additional $50 to get your license. If you are a temporary resident in the US, your license will expire at the end of your legal stay..

AAA

The American Automobile Association (AAA — people call it "Triple A") is a non-profit organization that you may want to join. Call (800) 222-4242 or enroll online at northeast.aaa.com/membership.html.

Members can call a 24-hour toll-free emergency telephone number, (800) 222-4357, anywhere in the US. AAA will send a repair or tow truck to you within one hour. The driver will:

- put a gallon of gas into your car
- change a flat tire
- re-start your car battery
- open your door if you have locked your keys inside
- tow your car to a garage

all free of charge (up to four times a year). In addition, some hotels give discounts to AAA members.

different traffic rules and driving habits, or if you are unfamiliar with driving in snow. Search on line for *Driving Instruction*, or ask a friend to help you pick a good company. If you are a licensed and experienced driver in your country, explain this to the instructor. You will take the lesson in the teacher's car. Ask if they have a teacher who speaks your language.

In Massachusetts, maximum speed limits vary from 55 to 65 miles per hour. Many international drivers think these speed limits are very low. Here's a bit of history. During the energy crisis of 1973, the US Congress passed an emergency national speed limit of 55 mph, in order to increase the average miles-per-gallon rate. In 1974, there were over 8,000 fewer highway deaths because of the lower speed limits. So even when that energy crisis passed, states continued the lower speed limit for many years. Now, the US Congress allows states to have higher speed limits. All but a few states do.

Getting a Driver's License

If you are a visitor to Massachusetts, not a resident, your home country license or international driver's license can be used for one year. Once you become a resident, you must get a Massachusetts driver's license within 30 days if you intend to drive here. Students should check with their International Student Office for rules applying to their visa status. You will find a local driver's license a useful and important form of identification. You must carry your license and car registration with you whenever you drive. With a Class D License, you may drive a car or small truck. You need a different license to drive a motorcycle, bus, large truck, or tractor.

The rules for getting a driver's license seem to change frequently and are not always applied evenly. Read the official Massachusetts Driver's Manual (available from a Registry of Motor Vehicles or on line at **www.massrmv.com.** See the box on page 53 for more details.

If you are from Canada or Mexico, you do not have to take the knowledge (written) or road tests. You must pay all fees and show a current certified driving record from your home country. If you are from one of the countries listed in the Convention on Road Traffic of 1949, you will have to take a written knowledge test, an eye test, and a road skills test. (Some international newcomers find that they are not required to take the road skills test if they have a valid license from their home country. You should plan to follow the rules, but do not be surprised if they seem to have changed!) You will probably have to give up your home country license.

Buying Gasoline for Your Car

You will find gas stations at busy corners, on main highways, and on toll roads; signs advertise their price per gallon. One US gallon is the same as 3.75 liters or .83 Imperial gallons. Each gas company has different grades of gas that differ in octane level, usually from 87 to 95. All gas (except diesel) sold in the US is unleaded. Companies name their levels differently, but you can choose by octane level - regular (87 octane), super, or plus (95 octane). Look in your car manual for the type of gas your car needs. Most gas stations only offer Self Service. Some only offer Full Service. Others offer both, at different pumps. The cost of gas at the Full Service pumps is slightly higher than the Self Service gas pumps. At Full Serve pumps, the attendant will

What to Do If a Police Officer Stops Your Car

- When you see the flashing lights behind you, stop your car on the side of the road as soon as it is safe.

- Do not get out of your car. Wait for the officer to come to your car. Then lower your window.

- The police officer will ask to see your driver's license and your automobile registration.

- Let the officer tell you why you were stopped.

- Cooperate and be courteous.

- Do not try to pay your fine in cash to the policeman. If he misunderstands you, he may think you are trying to bribe him. Pay all fines by mail or to the clerk of a court.

Once a police officer has stopped your car, he or she can look at anything in the car that is in plain view. However, officers can search the car (look in the trunk, under or inside boxes, etc.) only:

- if they see something that looks like a weapon, or

- if they have reason to believe you are hiding something illegal in the car, or

- if you give them your permission (say it is OK).

Always cooperate as much as possible with the officer.

Being Booted or Towed in the City of Boston

If you do not pay parking tickets, the city may put a 'boot' (clamp that prevents you from driving) on the wheel of your car. Before a booted vehicle is released, all outstanding parking violations issued to the owner, a $90 seizure fee, and any storage fees must be paid. Pay by cash, money order, cashier's check, or credit or debit card, but not personal check. If your car has not been towed, pay at the Office of the Parking Clerk, Room 224, 1 City Hall Plaza, Boston, Monday to Friday, 9 am to 4:30pm. They will remove the boot within 90 minutes or, if after 7pm, the next day.

Or, if your car has been towed, pay at the City of Boston Tow Lot, 200 Frontage Road, off the Southeast Expressway. Bring a valid driver's license with you. After you pay, the boot will be removed within about 90 minutes. Payments made after 4:30 pm may result in next day removal. You may have to pay a storage fee. Bring a valid driver's license with you. Call (617) 635-3900 with questions.

See how to dispute a charge at www.boston.gov/departments/parking-clerk

pump your gas, check your oil and radiator, and clean your windshields. You do not have to give the attendant a tip.

At Self Service pumps, you pump your own gas. You will find directions on how to pump your own gas on a sign at each pump. Usually you can choose to use a credit card at the pump or pay by cash inside the station before pumping; if you want to fill your tank, you will have to guess how much to pre-pay. The pump will stop automatically at the amount you have pre-paid or when the tank is full. If you have trouble, ask the attendant for help (even at a Self-Service station). You may clean your own windshield and check your own oil while you are there. There will be paper towels and a squeegee (window washing tool) next to the pump.

Parking your Car

Parking in Boston can be complicated and/or expensive, depending on where you live. Bostonians say, "The first parking space you see will be the last parking space you see." This might be a little bit exaggerated, but not too much! Always read the sign posts on the street before you park your car. Learn your community's special parking regulations. For example, in Brookline, parking is limited to 2 hours unless otherwise posted (and never overnight). You are expected to know the rules.

Places where you cannot park:
- Within ten feet of a fire hydrant
- In front of any curb ramp designed for use by handicapped persons
- In any place restricted by posted signs

Parking lots and garages. This is the safest,

but most expensive, way to park your car. Parking rates range from $3 to $25 per hour.

Meters. On different streets, there are different parking time limitations, varying from 15 minutes to 10 hours on any day other than a Sunday or legal holiday. Parking on these days is free. You cannot leave your car in a parking meter space beyond the time limit indicated on the parking meter. If the meter displays the message "Out of Order," you may not leave your car there longer than the maximum time allowed if the meter were working (or in Boston, for more than one hour).

Shopping area parking lots. Some stores have a parking lot for their customers. You can park only if you are shopping there. Pay attention to the time limit before you park your car.

Resident parking. If you see a "Resident Parking Only" sign posted, you cannot park unless your car has a Resident Parking Sticker for that neighborhood. If you ignore this sign, your car may get towed. To apply for a permit in Boston, visit **www.boston.gov/departments/parking-clerk/how-get-resident-parking-permit** or the Resident Parking Division at 1 City Hall Square, Room 224, Boston (617) 635-4410.

Overnight parking. In some parts of the Boston area, you may not park overnight on any street. The times of restriction differ from town to town. Ask your landlord or neighbors about this.

Street cleaning. On some streets marked with Street Cleaning signs, even those with Resident Parking permits must move their cars during the stated time so street-cleaning machines can clean the street.

If You Have an Accident in Your Car

Stop immediately. Exchange the following information with the other driver: name, address, driver's license number, car license plate number, car make, model, and year, car registration number, insurance company, and insurance policy number. Do not talk about who is at fault, even if you think it was you.

Call the police if:

- someone is hurt,
- you think there has been more than $1000 damage,
- one driver broke a traffic law that caused the accident, or
- the other driver refuses to give you the information about his registration and insurance.

In these cases, you must complete an accident report. Get an accident report form from any police station. Send the report, within five days, to the Registry of Motor Vehicles and to the Police Department in the town where the accident happened.

If the accident is serious, do not move your cars until the police come. The police will want to see the placement of the cars to understand what happened.

Vocabulary for Buying a New Car

Invoice Price: The standard car maker's price, paid by the dealer. But the dealer may have paid less than this standard price using special discounts.

Sticker Price: The retail price from the dealer. This price plus a list of all options and prices must be posted on a new car. This sticker also gives expected gas mileage.

Options: The extra features you may choose, like power door locks, power windows, or CD player.

Options Package: Car makers put some options together in a group and charge less for the group than if you bought each one separately. They may group options you want with options you don't.

Bargaining Space: The sticker price may be 10% to 20% higher than the invoice price. You and the dealer will negotiate a price within this range.

Special Order: If a dealer does not have the exact car you want, you may be able to make a special order. This will usually involve a delay, but you can get just the options you want. There is no extra charge for special orders.

If you get a parking ticket. If you return to your car and there is a ticket stuck to your window, do not throw it away! If you agree that you broke some parking rule, write a check and return the ticket and check to the Parking Clerk (see the ticket for instructions). To ensure proper credit, write your license plate number and ticket number on your payment. Or, for tickets in Boston, you can pay by with a credit card by telephone (617-635-4410), by mail or in person (1 City Hall Square, Room 224, Boston, MA 02201) or on-line (**www.boston.gov/departments/parking-clerk**). Other towns may also offer on-line payment. Look on your ticket to see if this is available.

If you think you have gotten a ticket unfairly (for example, if the meter was broken or the parking regulation sign was not visible), you may appeal it. See instructions on the ticket or call the town's parking clerk. You should write a letter explaining what happened, and/or go, in person, at an appointed time, to talk to the parking clerk. If you got a ticket because your car was broken, send a dated repair receipt, tow receipt or a copy of the police report along with a note of explanation.

If you ignore parking tickets, the police may tow your car to a secure lot, or attach a boot (clamp attached to one of your tires so you cannot drive it). See Sidebar page 56.

Buying, Leasing or Renting a Car

Know your facts about the car you would like. At your public library, newsstand, or on line, you can compare similar cars, learn about the many options, and compare prices. Boston can be hot in the summer, so you may want air conditioning and tinted windows. A car with front- or four-wheel drive will be handy in the winter snow.

To Buy a New Car

Buying a new or used car is one of the times in the US that you should try to bargain about the price of a product (offer a lower price than what the seller asks for). With very few exceptions, you can expect to pay a price that is lower than the advertised price.

To buy a new car, you will need to go to a car dealer. You may buy a used car either from a dealer or directly from the seller. Before you go to a dealer for a new car, it is useful to know the in-voice price (what the dealer paid the car maker). Sometimes the dealer will tell you. Or, you can read one of several New Car Buyers' Guides in the library or on line. They list the invoice prices for each model and each option. You can also visit the Federal Trade Commission for information at: **www.consumer.ftc.gov/articles/0209-buying-new-car**. For used cars, there are Used Car Buyers' Guides which give different prices for car models with different amounts of mileage.

Most people shop around, that is, go to or call a few dealers and ask each to give their "best price" for a new car. Then they go back to the dealer with the lowest price. Or they go to the dealer who has the best car available, and ask him to match the lowest price. Do not feel you have to buy from any dealer. It is fine to go home and think before you decide.

You will learn a lot when you begin to shop around. A good deal for one new car model may be $300 to $400 more than the dealer paid.

Massachusetts Safety Laws

Seat Belts

In Massachusetts, everyone in a car must wear a safety restraint. Children must ride in a federally-approved infant, toddler, or booster seat until they are at least 8 years old or 57 inches in height. Then, they (and adults) must wear a seat belt, whether they are in the front or back seat of the car.

Headlights

Massachusetts requires motorists to turn on their headlights and tail-lights whenever their vehicle's windshield wipers are used. Headlights and tail-lights must be turned on a half-hour after sunset and a half-hour before sunrise or when visibility is under 500 feet.

Cell Phones and Texting

Drivers under 18 years old are banned from using any mobile device for any reason while driving.

All drivers, regardless of age or license status, are banned from texting while behind the wheel.

Insurance for Your Car

Massachusetts car owners are required to have several kinds of insurance; other kinds are optional.

Required:

Bodily injury to others: for expenses of any person injured in any one accident.

Personal Injury Protection (PIP): medical and work loss expenses, no matter who is at fault.

Property damage: for injury to or destruction of someone else's property in any one accident.

Uninsured motorists: to cover costs if you are in an accident with an uninsured driver.

Optional:

Collision insurance: to pay for repairs to a car that has been hit in an accident.

Comprehensive insurance: to pay for repairs to the car that result for something other than a collision, like flood, theft, or fire.

Other models will be $500 to $1500 more than the dealer paid.

To Buy a Used Car

Public libraries, bookstores, and the internet will have books, magazines, and comparisons about repair histories and safety records of past car models. If you buy a used car from a dealer, there will be a Buyers' Guide sticker on the window of each car, required by law. The Buyers' Guide gives several general warnings on every car. For example, it tells what some common problems in all used cars are (not just this model). And it suggests that, before you buy the car, you should have the car inspected by a mechanic who is not connected to the dealer. In addition, it tells whether the car comes with a warranty, and if so, what the conditions of the warranty are. About half the used cars sold by dealers in the US come "as is" (with no warranty). If there is a problem, you have to pay for the repairs yourself. If the dealer promises to fix problems with a car you buy "as is," be sure to get the promises in writing. Or, the dealer may be selling the car with "implied warranties only." This is usually a very basic warranty that the car will run, and that it will do what the dealer says it will do. For example, if you say you need a car that can pull a trailer and the dealer recommends a particular car, the dealer is promising that it can pull the trailer. If you buy a used car directly from the seller, you probably will not have any warranty – it will be "as is." Have a mechanic look at it before you buy.

The dealer may, however, offer a "full" or "limited" warranty on a used car or on some of its systems (like the frame, body, or brake system). Limited warranties are most common; the limits differ from car to car. With a limited warranty, for example, you pay some of the costs of parts and labor if something goes wrong.

Some used cars may be marked as Certified Pre-Owned. This means that they meet certain age and mileage requirements set by the manufacturer and have passed a thorough inspection at the dealership. They may come with a manufacturer's (not just dealer's) warranty, allowing claims even if you move away from the dealer. There may be other advantages usually reserved for new cars (like lower financing rates). The exact meaning of this certification depends on the car. The certification comes with a price (from $300 to $2500), however, and in some cases it may not be worth the money. If you are sure that a car has been well-maintained and has a good reliability record, and you can get a good dealer warranty, the certification may not be necessary. See **www.edmunds.com/certified-cars/what-are-certified-used-vehicles.html** or **www. consumer.ftc.gov/articles/0055-buying-used-car** for more information.

To Lease a Car

Many people – international newcomers and Americans alike – decide to lease a car rather than buy one. There are some advantages and some disadvantages to leasing. On the positive side, with leasing you can get a new car with low monthly payments and little or no *down-payment* (money paid right away), repairs are covered by the car maker's warranty, and when the lease is over, you do not have the problem of selling a used car. If you have found a good deal, the overall cost (including the various fees and taxes) can be the same – or even lower – than buying a car with a loan (assuming that you would sell the

Vocabulary for Leasing a Car

Capitalized Cost: selling price of the new car. Ask what the "cap cost" is. The dealer may be using the sticker ("asking") price, but you can probably negotiate a lower one.

Acquisition and Disposition Fees: money you pay the leasing company at the beginning of the lease (Acquisition) and at the end of it (Disposition), to pay for their costs.

Money (or Lease) Factor: interest you pay, usually expressed as some small number; multiply that number by 24 to get the annual interest rate.

Residual Value: the estimated value of the car at the end of the lease.

Closed-end Lease (or Walk-Away Lease): you and the dealer agree on a Residual Value at the beginning of the lease. At the end, you can simply return the car and "walk away." If the car is actually worth less than expected, it is the dealer's problem, not yours. Most leases for individuals are closed-end.

Depreciation Fee: the amount of money the car will lose in value, divided by the number of months in the lease.

Buying a Car

www.edmunds.com
www.kbb.com
www.autobytel.com
www.cars.com
www.carbuyingtips.com
www.msn.com/autos

Leasing a Car

www.leaseguide.com
www.leasetips.com
www.leasecompare.com
www.leasespecials.com

Renting a Car

Alamo
www.alamo.com
(877) 222-9075

Avis
www.avis.com
(800) 331-1212

Budget
www.budget.com
(800) 527-0700

Dollar
www.dollar.com
(800) 800-4000

Enterprise
www.enterprise.com
(800) 261-7331

Hertz
www.hertz.com
(800) 654-3131

National
www.nationalcar.com
(800) 226-6890

Thrifty
www.thrifty.com
(800) 847-4389

car after the loan was paid). This is the case because new cars drop in value in the first several years – a $20,000 new car can be worth $13,000 after two years. With a lease, you are basically just paying for that $7,000 difference. However, consider the following:

• Most lease contracts include a strong penalty for ending the lease before the time is up. If you think there is a chance you will not finish the lease – for example, because you might return to your home country sooner than expected, or because you may need a larger car later – then leasing may not be the best choice for you.

• Lease contracts usually put a limit on the number of miles you can drive without paying extra. Limits of 12,000-15,000 are common. The limit may be acceptable to you. But if you are not used to the commute you face in the US, or if you plan a sight-seeing trip to California every year (3,000 miles each way), read this section of the lease carefully, too.

• You will have to pay the costs for repairs, except "wear & tear." Ask about what kind of maintenance is covered in your lease.

• You will probably need a Massachusetts driver's license before you can lease a car; international licenses are usually not accepted.

It is sometimes very hard to decide if a lease offer is a good one or not. Read about the different parts of the deal in the Sidebar in this chapter. Ask the dealer to tell you the capitalized cost, the fees, the interest rate, and the residual value – these all affect the financial deal. Ask for an unsigned contract from several dealers before you choose one. (Not all of them will do that for you, but it is fine to ask.)

To Rent/Share a Car for Short-Term Use

If you need a car for a short or temporary period of time, you might want to rent one. The major car rental companies have offices at Logan Airport as well as around the Boston area. For a list, see the Sidebar or check online for locations and telephone numbers of both major and smaller car rental companies. You may have to be at least 25 years old to rent a car; some companies will rent to 21-year-olds with a fee surcharge. You will find useful information at **www.bnm.com**.

Another option is shared cars. Shared cars are parked around the city. Members reserve cars on-line (see sidebar). They then go directly to the car, drive it away (using a key card) for as little as an hour, and then return it to the space by the reserved time. This service provides an alternative to car rentals, taxis, and car ownership, especially if you only need a car for a few hours every once in a while.

From City to City

Your visa allows you to travel freely within the US, so feel free to explore New England and the rest of the country. You can learn a lot of information about your destination and how to get there on-line. You can also buy your plane tickets and make car and hotel reservations on-line. However, if you don't have a US credit card, you may have a problem; some travel websites only accept credit cards with US billing addresses for payment. For this reason and others, many newcomers use a travel agent to help them plan a trip. A travel agent can make all your hotel, car, and airplane arrangements, especially if their

Shared Car Companies

Zipcar
www.zipcar.com

Enterprise CarShare
www.enterprisecarshare.com

Hertz
www.hertz247.com

On-Line Reservations

To make travel reservations (flight, hotel, car rental) on-line:

www.orbitz.com
www.expedia.com
www.travelocity.com
www.kayak.com
www.statravel.com
www.studentuniverse.com
www.cheaptickets.com
www.priceline.com
www.hotwire.com

Some of these sites charge a small fee for each reservation. You can also reserve directly on the sites of the airline, train or bus company or hotel.

Intercity Buses

Greyhound: Greyhound buses serve more than 2,500 destinations with 17,000 daily departures across the country. They have six stops in greater Boston. The main terminal is at South Station, 700 Atlantic Avenue. For more information, go to **www.greyhound.com**

Peter Pan: Peter Pan buses mainly serve Boston, New York, Philadelphia, Baltimore, and Washington but they also have service throughout Massachusetts. Their main terminal is at South Station, 700 Atlantic Avenue. For more information, go to **www.peterpanbus.com**

Boston-New York City: Greyhound and Peter Pan operate shared service to New York from Boston under the name **BoltBus**. Several other companies also offer frequent service.

Go to **www.newengland-travelplanner.com/transport/bus/bos_nyc_bus.html** for more information.

itinerary is complicated. You just tell them where you want to go, and they will tell you how they can help you. Most travel agents do charge a fee ($5 to $20) for their services, but there is no fee for information. For example, a travel agent can give you advice about interesting places to go, efficient ways to travel, and the visa and documentation you will need. Travel agents will usually accept a credit card with an international billing address, as well as debit cards and money orders, although most do not accept personal checks.

Intercity Buses

One way to travel from city to city is on an intercity bus. Some of these buses have on-board movies, snacks, and reclining seats. Information on intercity bus companies is in the Sidebar.

Train

Long distance train travel in the US is not as convenient or widely used as in many other countries. However you can easily take a train to New York City or Washington, DC and, from those cities, connect with other trains to go to other parts of the US. For schedules or to make a reservation, call (800) 872-7245 or visit **Amtrak.com**. There are four train stations in greater Boston:

South Station 700 Atlantic Avenue

North Station 126 Causeway Street

Back Bay Station 145 Dartmouth St

Route 128 Station 50 University Avenue

Air Travel

Whether you buy your airline tickets on your own or through a travel agent, remember a few key points:

- Different airlines charge different prices for

flights to the same city, and most airlines charge different prices for different seats on the same flight. Prices for the same flight may even vary from day to day. Shop around.

- Sometimes you get a better price when you buy your ticket two to three weeks before your trip or if you stay over a Saturday night.
- If you must travel during peak travel times (Thanksgiving in November, Christmas in December, Memorial Day in May, and July 4th) or any time over the summer, buy your tickets as far ahead as possible. Flights can sell out.
- Flights do get changed and cancelled. Especially if you have made your reservation very far in advance, double check the departure time on line. The airline will contact you by telephone or email if there are changes, so be sure to give them your contact information.
- Try to check in and print your boarding pass or save it on your smartphone 24 hours or less before the flight. This will save you time at the airport, especially if you do not have to check your suitcase.
- If you have not printed or saved your boarding pass, print one at the airport. Most airlines now offer self-serve check-in stations where you can print your pass. You will need your booking confirmation number, a credit card or your frequent flyer number to access your information

If you will be flying often while in the US, you may want to join the Frequent Flyer Club of one or more US airlines. If you already belong to one of these clubs from your home country, ask about whether that airline "partners" with any US airline. You should be able to continue to add miles to that account.

Public Transportation To and From Logan Airport

Logan Airport is three miles from downtown Boston. A taxi ride costs about $18-25. Or consider a 7-minute water shuttle from the Boston waterfront: www.massport.com/logan-airport/to-and-from-logan/water-transport.

The Blue Line of the MBTA has a station at the airport; take a free shuttle between the station and the airport. Connect from the Blue to Orange Line at State Street, or from Blue to Green at Government Center.

Or take the Silver Line (bus). These buses pick you up at each airport terminal (no need to shuttle to an MBTA station), and are free when traveling from the airport to South Station, including a free transfer to the Red Line. This is an especially good option if your destination is on the Red Line.

For up-to-date information about Logan airport, including available parking, weather conditions, construction projects that affect traffice, telephone numbers and terminal locations of each airline serving Logan airport, and more, see:

www.massport.com/logan-airport/to-and-from-logan/public-transportation/#silverline

Air Travel Web Sites

www.flightarrivals.com, www.flightview.com or flightaware.com/live. Expected arrival and departure times of all flights over the US and Canada. Or check Flight Status on your airline's webpage.

www.statravel.com or www.studentuniverse.com. Travel bargains for students and teachers.

www.flightstats.com. Extensive statistics on on-time arrivals by airline and airport, airline delays and cancellations all over the world.

www.seatguru.com. Click on your airline and type of plane to see a map of and comments about every seat on a plane.

www.farecompare.com/travel-advice/tips-from-air-travel-insiders. Lots of money-saving tips.

www.tsa.gov/traveler. Transportation Security Administration's site, if you have any questions about what you can take on the airplane or how you will be searched.

www.yapta.com. Track airfares for specific flights and buy when they're low.

For security reasons, adults must show government-issued identification with a photograph before getting on an airplane, including flights within the US. Visit www.tsa.gov for more information on travel safety regulations.

Ask your travel agent or check your airline's website for when you should plan to arrive at the airport. Security measures have made checking in for a flight more time-consuming. Generally if you already have your ticket and boarding pass and are flying within the US, you should be at the airport at least one hour before your flight, more if you are going to check luggage.

Airlines limit the number of carry-on bags allowed; rules differ from airline to airline, so ask about the rules when you make your reservation. Carry-on bags must fit over or under your seat. One carry-on bag and one personal item (purse or briefcase) are standard for most airlines.

If you are flying outside the US, you must check in at the ticket counter even if you have checked in on line (to show your passport) at least two hours before your flight departs. Be sure you understand your visa requirements for travel to other countries, and that you have the proper forms with your passport. Don't forget about transit visas. In some countries you need a visa just to change planes. All airports in the US follow international security guidelines.

Shopping

4 Tips for Making Choices in a US Supermarket

Many newcomers comment on the overwhelming number of choices they face in a US supermarket, even if they are used to shopping in large supermarkets. The new brands, each label needing translation, is a lot to manage. Here is some advice:

1 - First, ask if there are obvious differences among the brands you care about. How much sugar is in the cereal? Are there spices added to the canned tomatoes that you do not like?

2 - Then compare the brands that seem identical (or are different in ways you don't care about). Buy the least expensive one. This is often (but not always) the one with the supermarket's name on it. If you like it, ignore all the others in the future.

3 - If you do not like that choice, next time pick another one. Once you find a brand you like, ignore all the others. Write down the brand, the words, colors and pictures on the box. Take them with you each time, until you don't need this anymore.

4 - If two or more brands look identical to you, just close your eyes and pick one. The frustration comes if you think you have to test them all.

Shopping for Food

The Supermarket

Most people in the US shop for food at a supermarket. They shop once or twice a week, keeping the food in their large refrigerators and freezers. Of course, you do not have to shop this way. But the popularity of the supermarket explains a lot about how food is processed and sold in the US.

Most supermarkets are open seven days a week. Some are even open 24 hours a day (except between midnight Saturday and 8 am Sunday). See the Appendix of this book for the names of major stores in the area. Newer supermarkets tend to be bigger and to carry many kinds of products, not only food. At these supermarkets you can shop for plants, greeting cards, envelopes, socks, oil for your car, and medicines.

The most obvious thing about the newest supermarkets is how big they are. This means they can afford to offer many choices for each product. Each one claims to be the best. This can be very overwhelming, especially to newcomers who are shopping in a new language and new culture.

It is always a good idea to shop with a list. If possible, ask an American friend to go to the supermarket with you once. Focus on the foods that are most important to you. Ask the friend to translate the words you do not understand. And ask for advice about which brand to buy. Write down what you learn, including information about the brand, and the colors and picture on the box. Next time, shopping will be easier.

Or, if you are shopping alone, here's our advice: Ignore as many of the choices as you can! In one store, we once counted 124 different breakfast cereals, 203 different types of cookies, and 197 choices of salad dressings. Do not try to make the very best choice of every food — you will go crazy! Try the list of *4 Tips for Making Choices in a US Supermarket* in the Sidebar on the previous page.

What kinds of foods will you find in a supermarket? Some large stores have a fresh fish counter, a butcher, a deli, and a bakery. Many carry gourmet, organic, and/or imported products. The freshness of vegetables varies from store to store, even among those with the same name. Try several stores in your neighborhood, or ask a friend for a recommendation.

Most stores are organized in the same way. A sign hanging over each aisle tells you what is in the aisle. Generally, the fresh produce is the first section near the door. The frozen foods are usually the last.

If you cannot find something you want, ask at the Customer Service desk. (You can also ask anyone putting new food on the shelves, although sometimes these people work for the food manufacturer, not the store, and may not know the answer to your question.)

When you are ready to pay for your food, you must choose your checkout line. If you plan to pay with a check, you may have to have it approved at the Customer Service desk first. Some cashiers will only take cash. In some lines (Express Lanes), you can only buy 8 or 12 items. It can be very frustrating to wait in line and then

"I was paying for my groceries when the cashier said, "Paper or plastic?" I had no idea that she was asking what kind of bag I wanted. I was very embarrassed, and felt very stupid. Another time, the cashier said, 'Do you want cash back?' I had no idea what she was asking. We don't have debit cards in my country and I didn't know I could withdraw cash using my debit card when I pay at the supermarket."

International Shopping Areas

There are international markets all over Boston. **Bostonethnicmarkets. com** is a comprehensive list of ethnic markets and grocery stores in the Boston area. You can also find a concentration of some nationalities in the following areas:

Brighton and Brookline (on the Green B and C lines) — Kosher and Eastern European

Chinatown (downtown Boston, near the Boylston (Green Line), Chinatown (Orange Line), and Downtown Crossing (Red Line) T stops) — Chinese and other southeast Asian

East Cambridge (along Cambridge Street) — Portuguese and Brazilian

Jamaica Plain (Orange line) — Latin American and Caribbean

North End (downtown Boston, near Haymarket (Green or Orange Line) T stop) — Italian

Porter Square (north Cambridge, at Porter Square (Red Line) T stop) — Japanese

Watertown (Mt. Auburn Street) — Middle Eastern

find that you are in the wrong line. Most markets take credit cards and bank debit cards.

A store clerk will usually put your items into a bag for you. Of course, you may put your groceries into the bag yourself if you prefer. The clerk may ask you if you prefer a paper bag or a plastic one; some cities around Boston do not provide plastic bags. You can also bring your own bag, backpack, or cart to the supermarket for carrying your groceries home. Usually, you do not have to pay for your bag. Some stores offer a 5 cent discount if you provide your own bag. Many supermarkets now also sell reusable bags for around $1 each.

You may also want to use the automatic check out machines in some supermarkets, if you prefer to check out and bag your own groceries.

Health Food

More and more supermarkets are including health food (organically-grown, or "natural") items in their stores. Some stores even have entire aisles dedicated to the health-conscious shopper. Also, health food stores specializing in these natural and healthy products are growing in the Boston area. These stores often carry their own brand names (much like those in supermarkets) for a less expensive option. Dried food, such as grains and nuts, are often available to buy "in bulk" (you can buy as much or little as you want).

Specialty Food Stores

In addition to supermarkets, there are many smaller specialty food stores. Some offer only imported foods. Others (especially those further from the city) grow their own produce, so it is

Nutrition Label

By law, all food labels must include accurate information about what is in the food, in a way that is easy to read and easy to compare with similar products. The list of ingredients must be complete, and must be in order of amount (from most to least).

Nutrition Facts

Serving Size 2 oz (57g)

Amount per Serving

Calories 120   Calories from Fat 10

	% Daily Value*
Total Fat 1g	**2%**
Saturated Fat 0g	**0%**
Trans Fat 0g	
Cholesterol 0mg	**0%**
Sodium 210mg	**9%**
Total Carbohydrate 24g	**8%**
Dietary Fiber 1g	**4%**
Sugars 11g	
Protein 2g	

Vitamin A 0%	•	Vitamin C 4%
Calcium 2%	•	Iron 2%

* Percent Daily Values are based on a 2,000 calorie diet. Your daily values may be higher or lower depending on your calorie needs.

	Calories	2,000	2,500
Total Fat	Less than	65g	80g
Sat Fat	Less than	20g	25g
Cholesterol	Less than	300mg	300mg
Sodium	Less than	2,400mg	2,400mg
Total Carbohydrate		300g	375g
Dietary Fiber		25g	30g

Calories per gram

Fat 9 • Carbohydrates 4 • Protein 4

INGREDIENTS: Organic White Rice Flour, Oil, Vegetable, Canola, Organic Evaporated Cane Sugar, Eggs, Lemon juice, Soy Flour, Full-fat, Raw, Sugar, Powdered, Baking Powder, Salt, Table, Tapioca Flour, Nutmeg Ground

This information is about the product itself. It shows the amount of each nutrient in one serving (in g (grams) and mg (milligrams)). It also shows what percentage of the Daily Value (recommended amount) you will get in that serving, based on a daily diet of 2000 calories.

This information shows the amount of each nutrient recommended for 2000-calorie and 2500-calorie diets.

Buying Alcohol and Cigarettes

In the US, the sale of alcohol and tobacco is controlled by state governments. In Massachusetts, stores may sell alcohol from 8 a.m. to 11 p.m. Monday-Saturday, and 10a.m. to 11 p.m. on Sundays. Alcohol can only be sold in special stores that have a license. (Many stores and supermarkets do not have this kind of license.)

You must be 21 years old to buy alcohol, either in a store or restaurant/bar. The minimum age for buying tobacco is 18, although some cities in the state (like Boston) have a minimum age of 21. Expect to be asked to show official proof of your age when you buy either alcohol or tobacco. You can buy tobacco products in most convenience stores but pharmacies and stores on college campuses in Boston are not allowed to sell tobacco.

Restaurants must have a license to sell wine, beer, and alcoholic drinks. These licenses are expensive and, in some towns, difficult to get. You may be able to bring your own bottle of wine to a restaurant that does not have a license.

fresher. You will pay more, but you may decide the quality is worth the extra money.

Farms that Sell Their Own Produce

Most towns in the Boston area have farmers markets in the summer — farmers bring their produce to a market in the town center, usually once a week. Or, a few miles out of the city you will find farms that sell their own produce. Several of these farms invite people to pick their own fruit, too. Look for advertisements in the Boston Globe during the appropriate seasons. For example, pick strawberries in May and June, and apples in September. Because this is a popular family activity, plan to go at the beginning of the picking season. Go to **www. massfarmersmarkets.org** or **www.ams.usda. gov/FarmersMarkets** to learn about these options. CSAs (community supported agriculture) and Farm Shares are another source of locally grown food. Find CSA information at **www. mass.gov/agr/massgrown/csa_farms.htm**. Farms Shares, where you pay a set amount each week/monthly or semi-annually, provide you with a variety of produce delivered directly to you. More information is available at **metropedal-power.com/farmshare-delivery/**.

Shopping for Your Home

You will probably need to buy some things for your home — big things (like furniture), small things (like American measuring spoons or a wastebasket), or things in between (like a television or a window fan). Remember that electronics from your home country may not work in the US even with an adapter, and electronics you buy here may not work when you go home. Many newcomers to the United States do not want to spend a lot of money on these items. See the Appendix of this book for the names of major stores in the area. Here are some suggestions:

Moving Sales

Watch for informal signs near where you live for a "Moving Sale." People who are moving often sell all their furniture and housewares and you can often get very good prices.

Garage Sales

In the warm months, you will see signs advertising "garage sales" (also called "moving sales," "yard sales," "tag sales," or "barn sales"). People put out (in their garage, or yard, or barn) housewares, toys, clothes, and appliances that they no longer need or want. The prices are usually very low. The quality will range from excellent to awful. Sometimes several families or a church will join together to hold one of these sales — then the selection is large. These are sometimes called "flea markets." For example, for Davis Square in Somerville, see **thesomervilleflea.com.**

Additional information about open markets for artisans and craftspeople can be found at **new-englandopenmarkets.com.**

Craigslist

Craigslist.org is a website where people can advertise furniture or other items they would like to sell or give away. Contact the seller directly and arrange to see the item. You should be careful about scams, but many people find bargains this way. Learn more about recognizing scams at **www.craigslist.org/about/scams**.

"When we first arrived we needed new furniture. When I looked through the newspaper, I found a big SALES advertisement. I decided to go immediately because I thought this was my last chance to get good quality furniture for a good price. In my country we have sales twice a year but here I soon learned that the stores can announce a sale and offer selected merchandise at a reduced price, or mark down merchandise of a lesser quality, and that sales are year round!"

On-line Shopping

Books

www.amazon.com (also sells many other kinds of products)
www.half.ebay.com
www.ecampus.com
www.barnesandnoble.com
www.abebooks.com

Groceries

www.peapod.com
www.groceries-express.com
www.instacart.com
(provides items from many different stores)

Almost all major super-markets have proprietary delivery services.

Online Auctions

www.ebay.com
www.ubid.com

Newspaper Advertisements

You can sometimes find larger items (like furniture and cars) advertised in the Classified Section of your local newspaper. Because there is no store involved, prices may be low. Look for Want Ads, which are person-to-person sales.

Charity Organizations and Thrift Stores

There are several charity organizations that accept used furniture, clothes, and appliances from people who do not need them, then sell them at low prices. The profits go to the charity. Examples are Goodwill Industries and the Salvation Army. These organizations are good to remember, both now and when you want to give furniture or clothes away. You may take a charity tax deduction for the value of the items you give.

Discount Stores

Look for discount stores (sometimes called "outlets") that sell brand name items at discounted prices. For example, if a brand name washing machine costs $550 at a regular store, you may be able to find the same washing machine at a discount store for $490. Some discount stores specialize in what they sell — home appliances, clothing, shoes, electronic equipment, computers, food, etc.

Department Stores

Department stores sell a variety of items, including furniture and housewares (kitchen items, bath towels, bed linens). Watch for their sales — often at holiday times like Labor Day or Memorial Day — to get bargains.

Furniture Rental Stores

You may choose to rent furniture rather than

bring it from home or buy it in the US. Generally, it is more expensive to rent things like carpets, televisions, and stereo equipment than it is to buy them, especially if you will be here more than one year.

Internet and Catalog Sales

Many Americans do a lot of their shopping on line or mail-order catalog. The advantages, compared to shopping in a store, are:

- you can shop at odd hours,
- you don't have to travel from store to store,
- you can shop without your children, and
- you're more likely to find the item you want in the color and size you want, than in a store.

The disadvantage, of course, is that you cannot see and feel the item before you buy it. Catalog companies are usually very good about taking things back if you don't like them, but that is inconvenient.

For catalog shopping, you can usually order by telephone, fax, Internet or mail. Telephone is fastest, but if you feel unsure of your English, use the fax, Internet, or mail. If you use the telephone, make your choices before you call. Each item will have an "item number" next to it in the catalogue — have this ready. Also, if you use the phone, you will have to pay by credit card; have your card number ready.

Most purchases have an added "shipping and handling" charge, so the item really costs more than the price next to it. Usually, if you want faster delivery, you can pay more money to get it. Some companies offer free shipping with larger orders. Amazon.com offers a Prime program: pay $99/

Women's Clothing Sizes

Women's clothing sizes are quite variable in the US. Just because you are a size 10 in one store or from one designer does not mean size 10 will always fit you.

Most clothing stores use a sizing system from 0 to 16 for their main lines. See the Appendix for a comparison with sizing from other countries.

Other stores use the concepts of "Small," "Medium," or "Large:"

XS = extra small (size 0-4)
S = small (size 4-8)
M = medium (size 8-10)
L = large (size 10-14)
XL = extra large (size 16)

Still other stores or designers may have their own system, for example, "0, 1, 2, 3."

See more, including size comparisons for women, men and children, in the Appendix to this book.

year then get free 2-day (or faster) shipping for free.

You will usually be allowed to return an item, for any reason. Even if you simply don't like it, or have changed your mind, you should be able to return it. If something is wrong with the item (it is broken or not the color you ordered), the company should pay for the postage to return it. Some companies will pay for returns for any reason. If you want them to pay, read the catalog for instructions or call the Customer Service number on the catalog — they will tell you their policy. When the company receives the returned item, you will get your money back. You are under no obligation to pay for the fastest postage to return the package or to insure it against loss (but you will not receive your money until the company receives it safely).

Shopping Malls and Centers

Boston has many shopping malls and centers where you will find many stores, usually under one roof. The Box on the next page lists some of the largest ones.

Shopping Malls

Arsenal Project
485 Arsenal Street
Watertown, MA
arsenalyards.com

Burlington Mall *
Exit 32B off Route 128
75 Middlesex Turnpike #1
Burlington, MA

Cambridgeside Galleria
100 Cambridgeside Place
Cambridge, MA
www.cambridgeside.com

Mall at Chestnut Hill *
199 Boylston Street
Chestnut Hill, MA

Colonial Shopping Mall
85 River Street
Waltham, MA
colonial-shopping-center.hub.biz

Copley Place *
100 Huntington Avenue
Boston, MA

Dedham Mall
300 Providence Highway
Dedham, MA
www.dedham-mall.com

Downtown Crossing
Washington Street
Boston, MA
www.downtownboston.org

Emerald Square *
999 S. Washington Street
North Attleboro, MA

Faneuil Hall & Quincy Market
1 Faneuil Hall Square
Boston, MA
www.faneuilhallmarketplace.com

Fresh Pond Mall
545 Concord Avenue
Cambridge, MA

Greendale Mall *
7 Neponset Street
Worcester, MA

Hanover Mall
1775 Washington Street
Hanover, MA
www.hanovermall.com

Kingston Collection
101 Kingston Collection Way
Kingston, MA
www.kingstoncollection.com

Legacy Place
680 Legacy Place
Dedham, MA
legacyplace.com

Liberty Tree Mall *
100 Independence Way
Danvers, MA

Meadow Glen Mall
3850 Mystic Valley Prkway
Medford, MA
www.meadowglen.com

Natick Mall
1245 Worcester St.
(Route 9) Natick, MA
www.natickmall.com

Northshore Mall *
Routes 128 and 114
Peabody, MA

Prudential Center
800 Boylston Street
Boston, MA
www.prudentialcenter.com

Shopper's World
1 Worcester Rd. (Route 9)
Framingham, MA
ddr.com/properties/a21422

Silver City Galleria
2 Galleria Mall Drive
Taunton, MA
www.silvercitygalleria.com

South Shore Plaza *
250 Granite Street (Route 37)
Braintree, MA

Square One Mall *
1201 Broadway
Saugus, MA

The Village Shoppes
95 Washington Street
Canton, MA
www.villageshoppes-canton.
com

Watertown Mall
550 Arsenal Street
Watertown, MA
www.watertown-mall.com

Westgate Mall
200 Westgate Drive
Brockton, MA
www.shopatwestgatemall.
com

Wrentham Village Premium Outlets *
1 Premium Outlets Blvd.
Wrentham, MA

* Information about this mall can
be found at www.simon.com

Notes

Daily Life

Cooking Measures

boiling water = 212°F = 100°C

freezing = 32°F = 0°C

moderate oven = 350°F = 180°C

normal body = 98.6°F = 37°C

1 cup flour = 140 grams

1 cup sugar = 200 grams

1 pound = .45 kilograms

1 kilogram = 2.2 pounds

3 teaspoons (t) = 1 tablespoon (T)

16 tablespoons (T) = 1 cup (C)

2 tablespoons (T) liquid = 1 ounce (oz)

¼ cup (C) = 2 ounces (oz)

1 pint = 2 cups

1 quart = 2 pints = 4 cups

1 gallon = 4 quarts

"pinch" = less than 1/8 teaspoon

"dash" = a few drops

"stick" of butter = 1/4 pound

whole milk = at least 3.25% fat

low-fat milk = 0.5 to 2.0% fat

skim or nonfat milk = less than 0.1% fat

half-and-half = 10.5-18% fat

light coffee cream = 18-30% fat (cannot be whipped)

light whipping cream = 30-36% fat

heavy (whipping) cream = 36% fat

sour cream = 18% fat

Cooking in a US Kitchen

If you live in a part of Boston that has many other residents from your country, you may be able to find food and utensils that will allow you to cook the way you are used to at home. However, you will surely find that there are important differences — the oil tastes different, the stove does not heat the same way, you cannot find the right spices. Here is some information to get you started in an American kitchen:

Ovens. Most ovens in the US have two settings: Bake and Broil. When you choose Bake, the heat comes from the bottom coils only. When you choose Broil, the heat comes from the top coils only. Choose Bake and put the food in the middle rack of the oven if you want the food to be surrounded by heat. Choose Broil and put the food on the top or second rack if you want intense, fast heat on one side of the food only (for example, to cook fish or meat). With Broil, you will have to turn the food over half way through the cooking time. Also, leave the door open a few inches or the food will be baked too by the surrounding heat (your oven door will have a notch to keep it open a few inches).

Electric Stoves. An American electric stove may be difficult to cook on if you are used to different voltage, or to cooking with gas. It may heat or cool more slowly. Watch your food closely until you get used to this kind of stove.

Microwave Oven. Microwave ovens are a quick and convenient alternative to cooking with a conventional oven. You can use a microwave's programmed buttons to prepare or defrost certain foods quickly (for example, frozen pizza).

Most plates and dishes are safe for use in microwaves, but you should never put anything metal in your microwave.

Refrigerators. The large American refrigerators and freezers reflect a lot about American life. Because Americans often shop only once a week, the food they buy is designed to last a week, especially if refrigerated or frozen. They put some foods in the refrigerator that you might leave out, so that it lasts the whole week. Many Americans buy fish or meat that is on sale at a discount, then freeze it until they need it.

Measurements. You can buy an inexpensive measuring cup and set of measuring spoons at a supermarket. You will need them (and the measurement information found in the Sidebar) if you try to follow an American recipe. If you want a scale to weigh food, you may have to go to a gourmet kitchen shop, as scales are not usually used by Americans.

Laundry

Unless you have an apartment with its own clothes washer and dryer, you will probably wash your clothes in coin-operated machines at a neighborhood laundromat or in the basement of your apartment building. The advantage of a laundromat is that you can often do several loads of clothes at once, saving time. Here are a few tips in case washing clothes in these kinds of machines is new for you:

- In most laundromats you will need quarters (25¢ coins) for most machines. Collect them as you go through your daily life so you have

Cross-Unit Equivalents

US recipes often list food measured in cups even though, in the stores, the food is sold by the pound (1 pound = .45 kilograms). This will get you started:

3½-4 cups all-purpose flour = 1 pound
4¼ cups whole wheat flour = 1 pound
3 cups shelled almonds, peanuts, or walnuts = 1 pound
2 cups white sugar = 1 pound
2¼ cups brown sugar (packed tight) = 1 pound

Postal Rates for Letters

Within US

First Class Mail:

postcards: 35¢

letters: < 1 ounce (oz): 50¢;
1-2 oz 71¢; 2-3oz 92¢;
3-3.5 oz $1.13; large
envelopes start at $1.00
for <1oz

Priority Mail (1-3-day delivery): $6.70 for a flat rate
envelope; other prices
vary by weight, package
size and distance.

Running late? Try **Express
Mail** ($21.98) for flat
rate envelope. Other
prices vary by weight,
package size and distance. Can ship up to 70
pounds)

International

airmail letters: up to 1
ounce $1.15

Quicker delivery is also available through Priority or
Express Mail International. Check the web
sites below or ask at a
Post Office.

**www.usps.com
ircalc.usps.gov**
(international rates)
postcalc.usps.gov
(domestic rates)

enough or use the change machines in the laundromat. Each machine load will require several quarters.

- Sometimes laundromats sell small boxes of laundry detergent, but these are more expensive than large boxes from the supermarket.

- Wash different-colored clothes separately. You may have a white, a light-colored, and a dark-colored load. Or separate by colors (whites, red/pink, light and dark blue, etc).

- Hot water gets clothes cleanest but may shrink your clothes. A hot dryer also shrinks some fabrics, like wool. Read the labels carefully.

- Clothing labels may say "Dry Clean Only." It is safest to take their advice although some fabrics can be hand-washed. Also, there are now products available so you can clean these clothes in your own dryer.

- If your washing machine has a Delicate setting, you may be able to wash clothes labeled "Hand Wash Only." Use cold water and special soap made for woolen and delicate material. Even if you use the machine to wash, you may want to dry the clothing "flat" (lying on a table so it does not stretch) or on a hanger rather than in a dryer.

- Do not over-fill the washer or dryer. If you do, your clothes will not get clean and/or will be very wrinkled.

- Remove clothes from the washer and dryer immediately, to reduce wrinkles (and as a courtesy to other people waiting for the machines).

For more laundry tips, see:

www.automaticlaundry.com/laundry-tips.html.

US Postal System

Mail is delivered to homes six days each week, Monday through Saturday. There is no mail delivery on federal (US-government) holidays, because the post office is a federal agency. You will find a Post Office in every town. The US Postal Service offers many services. If you have a specific question call or visit the Post Office. Some USPS offices offer a 24-hour automated kiosk where you can buy stamps and mail

The Forever Stamp

All first class stamps issued by the USPS are 'Forever Stamps'. They do not have a monetary value printed on them. Currently forever stamps costs $.50 for domestic mail or $1.15 for international mail. If there is a price increase, existing forever stamps will still be valid for a first class letter of one ounce, no matter what you paid for it.

MARY SMITH
123 MAIN STREET
TOWN, MA 12345

PROFESSOR JOHN JOHNSON
456 HIGH STREET
CITY MA 12345

How to address an envelope

Write your name and address in the upper left corner. Write your friend's name and address in the center. Put the five- or nine-digit zip code on the same line as the city and state. Use the official 2-letter state abbreviations (see Sidebar on page 85). For letters going outside the US, write the name of the country on a separate line at the bottom; write it in English and use all capital letters. The stamp goes in the upper right corner. The Post Office prefers you to use all capital letters and no punctuation in all parts of the address and return address, so its equipment can read it more easily.

Postal Security Options

Certified Mail: You get a receipt that your letter was mailed at the post office. Use this if you want to be able to prove that you mailed something. $3.35

Insurance: If you insure your mail and it gets lost, the insurance will pay you cash. Starts at $2.10

Return Receipt: Use this service if you want proof that the mail was delivered. You will get a receipt showing the time and date of delivery and the signature of the person who received it. This service is available only if you order other security safeguards as well. $2.75 for mailed receipt; $1.45 for emailed receipt.

Registered Mail: You get confirmation that you mailed the item and that it was delivered (or at least that a delivery attempt was made). This is the maximum protection and security offered. Rates differ with the value of mail and whether or not you also buy insurance. Starts at $11.70

See more details and options at www.usps. com/ship/insurance-extra-services.htm

packages. Check your local office to see if it is equipped with one of these.

It is helpful to the letter carrier if you put a small sign with your last name(s) next to your doorbell or mail box. This lets the letter carrier know you have moved in.

To compute the cost of domestic mail, go to **postcalc.usps.gov;** for international mail, go to **ircalc.usps.gov**.

Speed of mail delivery. The Post Office says that most first class mail within the US takes 3-4 business days to arrive. Mail within one city takes one to two days. Or you can use Priority Mail to major cities in the US. Priority Mail "strives for" (but does not guarantee) delivery within 2-3 days. For overnight delivery, the US Post Office offers Express Mail. Or try a private company like Federal Express (**www.fedex.com**) or UPS (**www.ups.com**).

First class international mail to other countries (both letters and packages) is supposed to take 7-10 days. Surface mail takes from 4-12 weeks, depending on the distance and the delivery system in the other country. Global Priority Mail, offered to over 40 countries, is faster than first class (6-10 days), and Express Mail International (3-5 days), available to 180 countries and territories, is the fastest.

Mail delivery within the US is generally thought to be safe from theft and loss. But you may want to use one of several security safeguards for valuable items (see Sidebar on this page).

Boston's Weather

Here are some tips for living in a Boston winter:

1) Do not turn your home heat off when you go away in the winter. If you do, the water pipes may freeze and break. This may cause thousands of dollars of damage. To save energy, it is safe to turn your thermostat down a bit when you go away, but never allow the pipes to freeze.

2) The heat in some apartment buildings is centrally controlled; you will not be able to turn the furnace on or off by yourself, although you may be able to make it higher or lower by turning a thermostat or adjusting the radiator. Ask your landlord to show you how yours works. Do not be alarmed if you hear funny noises coming from the heat — many older systems make clanging and banging sounds.

3) If you are not used to driving in the snow and ice, consider taking a driving lesson from a licensed driving school (look online). A teacher can teach you how to apply your brakes and how to get in and out of parking spots in the snow. Tell the teacher that you are an experienced driver, but have never driven in snow.

4) Prepare your car for freezing weather. A car's problems tend to get worse in the cold weather. Ask a friend or neighbor for the name of a good mechanic. Some additional tips:

- Give your car a tune-up if it has not had one recently.
- In cold weather, your battery loses some of its power, so be sure your battery is strong.
- Tire pressure also drops with cold weather,

State Abbreviations

Alabama	AL
Alaska	AK
Arizona	AZ
Arkansas	AR
California	CA
Colorado	CO
Connecticut	CT
Delaware	DE
District of Columbia	DC
Florida	FL
Georgia	GA
Hawaii	HI
Idaho	ID
Illinois	IL
Indiana	IN
Iowa	IA
Kansas	KS
Kentucky	KY
Louisiana	LA
Maine	ME
Maryland	MD
Massachusetts	MA
Michigan	MI
Minnesota	MN
Mississippi	MS
Missouri	MO
Montana	MT
Nebraska	NE
Nevada	NV
New Hampshire	NH
New Jersey	NJ
New Mexico	NM
New York	NY
North Carolina	NC
North Dakota	ND
Ohio	OH
Oklahoma	OK
Oregon	OR
Pennsylvania	PA
Rhode Island	RI
South Carolina	SC
South Dakota	SD
Tennessee	TN
Texas	TX
Utah	UT
Vermont	VT
Virginia	VA
Washington	WA
West Virginia	WV
Wisconsin	WI
Wyoming	WY

School Closing Reports

Schools and universities may close during snowstorms if school officials think traveling to school will be unsafe for students and teachers. To learn whether your school is closed, listen to one of these radio or television stations after 6:15 am:

WBZ   1030 AM
WBUR   90.9 FM TV
channels   4, 5, 7

Or go to one of these sites:
www.wbz.com
www.whdh.com
www.wcvb.com

Weather Forecasts

www.boston.com/section/
   weather
www.weather.com
www.wunderground.com
www.weather.gov

so check yours (for free at most gas stations) once the weather gets cold.

- Never put plain water in your radiator - it may freeze and crack the radiator. Use a mixture of half water and half antifreeze instead; the liquid will not freeze until it is -37°C. Start with a fresh mixture every two years.

- Have plenty of washer fluid (not water — it will freeze) in your tank to clean the windshield.

- Whether you need special snow tires or chains depends on (a) how much snow falls, (b) the kinds of roads you travel, (c) whether the roads will be cleared by snow plows, and (d) the kind of car you drive. Ask your mechanic and neighbors to help you decide.

Consulates

Many countries have a consulate in the Boston area. If you have questions or need help from your home country, be sure to contact them. (See list on page 88). Since some of these are "honorary consulates" you may need to contact your country's U.S. embassy for additional assistance.

News

Local newspapers provide valuable information about local news and activities. Boston has two major city-wide newspapers (The Boston Globe and The Boston Herald). Each town also has at least one local paper. Look on newsstands around your community, then call to ask about having the paper delivered. Some town news-

Temperature Chart

Temperatures	Jan	Feb	Mar	Apr	May	Jun	Jul	Aug	Sep	Oct	Nov	Dec	Total
Maximum Celcius (°C)	2	4	8	13	19	25	28	27	23	17	11	6	15
Minimum Celcius (°C)	-6	-4	-1	5	10	15	18	18	14	8	3	-2	7
Maximum Fahrenheit (°F)	36	39	46	55	66	77	82	81	73	63	52	43	59
Minimum Fahrenheit (°F)	21	25	30	41	50	59	64	64	57	46	37	28	44

Rainfall/Precipitation Chart

Rainfall	Jan	Feb	Mar	Apr	May	Jun	Jul	Aug	Sep	Oct	Nov	Dec	Total
Rainfall (mm)	91	91	94	91	81	79	71	81	79	84	107	102	1051
Rainfall (inches)	3.6	3.6	3.7	3.6	3.2	3.1	2.8	3.2	3.1	3.3	4.2	4.0	41
Boston Days of Rain	12	10	12	11	12	11	9	10	9	9	11	12	128

Snowfall Chart

Snowfall	Jan	Feb	Mar	Apr	May	Jun	Jul	Aug	Sep	Oct	Nov	Dec	Total
Snowfall (mm)	325	300	203	23	0	0	0	0	0	0	33	193	1077
Snowfall (inches)	12.8	11.8	8.0	0.9	0	0	0	0	0	0	1.3	7.6	42

Seasonal Chart

Snowfall	Average Temp				Total Rainfall			
	(Max °C)	(Min °C)	(Max °F)	(Min °F)	(mm)	(inches)	(mm)	(inches)
Mar to May (Spring)	13	5	56	40	266	11	226	9
Jun to Aug (Summer)	27	17	80	62	231	9	0	0
Sept to Nov (Autumn / Fall)	17	8	63	47	270	11	33	1
Dec to Feb (Winter)	4	-4	39	25	284	11	818	32

Consulates in Boston Area

Offices are in Boston unless listed otherwise. For more, see www.embassypages.com/city/boston

Albania
162 Boylston St.
(617) 482-2002

Austria*
15 School St., Fl. 5
(617) 227-3131

Belgium*
18 Washington Sq West
Salem
(978) 825-4300

Brazil
20 Park Plaza # 810
(617) 542-4000

Bulgaria*
2 Newton Pl #300
Newton
(617) 219-1490

Cambodia*
93 Chelmsford Street
Lowell
(978) 735-4539

Canada
3 Copley Place, # 400
(617) 247-5100

Cape Verde
300 Congress St. #204
Quincy
(617) 353-0014

Chile*
1 Bernard O'Higgins Cr
Brighton
(617) 232-0416

Colombia
31 St.James Ave.,# 960
(617) 536-6222

Czech Republic*
28 Howe Street
Wellesley
(617) 358-1776

Denmark*
1165R Mass Ave #101
(617) 542-1415

Dominican Republic
20 Park Plaza #601
(617) 482-8121

Ecuador*
52 Cranberry Lane
Needham
(781) 400-1212

El Salvador
46 Bennington St,
(617) 567-8338

Finland*
101 Arch St., Fl. 19
(617) 939-9542

France
31 St. James Ave., #750
(617) 832-4400

Georgia
17 Berkley Street
Cambridge
(617) 492-0727

Germany
3 Copley Place, #500
(617) 369-4900

Greece
86 Beacon St.
(617) 523-0100

Haiti
545 Boylston St., #201
(617) 266-3660

Hungary*
111 Huntington Ave.
(617) 342-4022

Iceland*
225-B Merrimac Street
Woburn
(781) 938-1820

Ireland
535 Boylston St. 5th Fl.
(617) 267-9330

Israel
20 Park Plaza, #1020
(617) 535-0201

Italy
600 Atlantic Ave. #1700
(617) 722-9201

Jamaica*
183 State Street, #6
(617) 778-0021

Japan
600 Atlantic Ave., Fl. 22
(617) 973-9772

S. Korea
300 Washington St #251
Newton
(617) 641-2830

Lebanon*
366 N. Main Street
Andover
(978) 289-4142

Luxembourg*
185 Franklin Street
(617) 772-1399

Malta
56 Lantern Road
Belmont
(617) 484-1731

Mexico
55 Franklin St, Ground Fl
(617) 426-4181

Monaco
40 Broad Street
(617) 226-9797

Morocco
moroccanconsulate
boston.com

Nicaragua*
52 Mulberry St
Springfield
(413) 739-0801

Norway*
326 A St. #2C
(617) 423-2515

Pakistan*
1032 Main St. # 5
Millis
(617) 267-9000

Peru
20 Park Plaza, #511
(617) 338-2227

Poland*
22 Pratt Ct.
Cohasset
617-357-1980

Portugal
699 Boylston St.,7th Fl.
(617) 536-8740

Romania*
Harvard Square
Cambridge
(617) 497-1111

Rwanda
151 Tremont St #21K
(617) 948-9449

Slovakia*
3 Round Hill Road
Weston
(781) 647-1674

Spain
31 St. James St., #905
(617) 536-2506

Sweden*
326 A Street #2C
(617) 451-3456

Switzerland*
420 Broadway
Cambridge, MA
(617) 876-3076

Taiwan Trade Office
99 Summer St. #801
(617) 259-1350

Thailand*
41 Union Street
(617) 720-8424

Turkey
31 St. James #840
(617) 451-1329

United Arab Emirates
1 International Pl #2901
(617) 948-8800

United Kingdom
One Broadway
Cambridge
(617) 245-4500

Venezuela
545 Boylston St., 3rd Fl.
(617) 266-9368

* Honorary consulate. May not offer regular consular services such as passport replacement, issuing visas, legal assistance, document certification, and other general assistance.

papers are free. There are also free city-wide newspapers, such as Boston Metro. Check the Sidebar for on-line ways to get US national news, international news, and news from your home country.

Studying English

You may want to study English while you live in Boston. Almost every town in the Boston area offers lessons at libraries or community centers and/or has language schools and tutors. A few in the city of Boston are listed on the next page.

News Sources

TV Stations: Every broadcast TV station has daily news (see chapter on Connecting to the World)

The Boston Globe: to subscribe, call 1 (888) 694-5623 or go to: www.bostonglobe.com/subscribers/ Student rates and digital subscriptions available.

The Boston Herald: to subscribe, call (800) 882-1211 or go to: www.bostonherald.com/about/subscribe Student rates and digital subscriptions available.

New York Times: to subscribe call (800) 698-4637 or go to: www.homedelivery.nytimes.com Student rates and digital subscriptions available.

Local Newspapers: For a list of town papers and to subscribe, go to: www.usnpl.com/manews.php Some are free.

Newspapers Around the World: www.allnewspapers.com

On Line News: www.cnn.com www.reuters.com news.google.com news.yahoo.com

Places to Study English

Here are some places in Boston to study English. Each town also has schools. For more classes, see www.cityofboston.gov/newbostonians/search.asp

Approach International Student Center
196 Harvard Ave., #2, Allston
(617) 787-5401 (c)
approachusa.org

Asian American Civic Asscn.
87 Tyler St., Boston
(617) 426-9492 (c)
aaca-boston.org/programs-services/english-language-classes/

Asian Student Center
1106 Commonwealth Ave., Boston
(617) 730-3706
www.aplusprogram.com/

Boston Academy of English
38 Chauncey St. 8th floor, Boston
(617) 338-6243 (c/i)
www.bostonacademyofenglish.com

Boston Ctr. for Adult Education
122 Arlington St., Boston
(617) 267-4430 (c)
www.bcae.org

Boston Language Institute
648 Beacon St., Boston
(617) 262-3500 (c/i)
www.bostonlanguage.com

Boston School of Modern Languages
814 South St, Boston
(617) 325-2760 (c/i)
www.bostonschoolofenglish.com/en/

Boston Univ Ctr for English Language
890 Commonwealth, Boston
(617) 353-4870 (c)
www.bu.edu/celop

Inlingua
31 St. James Ave. #805, Boston
(617) 542-6777 (i)
www.inlinguaboston.com

International Institute of Boston
1 Milk St. #4, Boston
(617) 695-9990 (c)
iine.org

JVS American Language Program
75 Federal Street, 3rd Floor, Boston
(617) 399-3131 (c)
www.jvs-boston.org

Kaplan International
540 Commonwealth Ave, Boston
39 JFK Street, Cambridge
(c/i)
www.kaplaninternational.com/united-states/boston

Northeastern University English Language Center
360 Huntington Ave., Boston
(877) 668-7727 (c)
cps.northeastern.edu/programs/international/language-prep

YMCA Boston-International Learning Center
3 Center Plaza #901, Boston
(617) 927-8244 (c)
www.ymcaboston.org/internationallearningcenter

Key:
c = classroom
i = individual
im = immersion
in = intensive

Medical Concerns

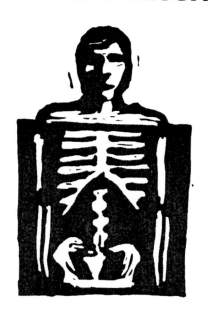

Here are some questions to ask about your medical insurance:

- Do you have to choose a doctor from your insurance company list, or can you choose any doctor you like?

- What services are covered? Do you have to pay part of the fee for visits to the doctor? for laboratory tests? for surgery? for hospital fees? If so, how much? Is there an upper limit to what the insurance company will pay?

- Do you pay for doctor services and tests yourself, then mail an insurance claim, or should the doctor send the bill directly to the insurer?

- What kind of approval from the insurance company do you need before you get any services?

- What should you do if you need medical care when you are out of town? out of the US?

- Does your policy pay for prescriptions?

- Does your policy pay for mental health counseling? dental work? vision services?

Getting Medical Care

Massachusetts law requires all residents to have health insurance. Government-funded insurance is available for low-income residents, and low-cost options are available to residents who do not get health insurance from their employers. Commonwealth Connector is the state agency managing new mandatory health insurance. To enroll, call (877)-MA-ENROLL (1-877-623-6765), or go to **www.mahealthconnector.org**.

Be sure that you understand how your insurance works before anyone gets sick. Policies vary widely from company to company. The Sidebars in this chapter suggest some questions to ask about your insurance, and define some words you will hear.

University Health Centers
Most students go to their university health center if they are sick. If they need to be seen somewhere else, the health center will give directions.

Choosing a Doctor
In the US, most routine medical care is provided either by a family (or general) practitioner who will care for your whole family, or a pediatrician for children and an internist for adults. If you need to see another kind of specialist, your general physician will suggest names for you. In many doctors' offices, a nurse, nurse practitioner, or physician's assistant may also give you care. These professionals have training in routine medical care and, in some cases, may be able to prescribe medicines and do simple procedures.

There are several ways to choose a doctor. Probably the best way is to ask your friends or neighbors for a recommendation. You can also check **bostonmagazine.com/top-doctors** or **www. healthgrades.com** for additional suggestions. It is a good idea to make an appointment with a doctor while you are healthy, to see if you feel comfortable with her/him. In the US it is common and acceptable to interview a prospective doctor before you choose one. Make an appointment with several doctors and discuss your needs with each one. You will soon find out which doctor is sensitive to your philosophy of care. If you have brought medical records with you, leave a copy of them with the doctor you choose.

Getting Health Care When You Need It

In the US, doctors rarely make house calls. You must go to the doctor's office (or student health center), no matter how ill you are. Once you have chosen a doctor, you can telephone his or her office when you are sick. The doctor or the nurse will ask you questions and the two of you will decide if you should go to the doctor's office.

If you get sick before you have a doctor, but it is not an emergency, here are some options:

- Many towns have neighborhood walk-in clinics. These may be run by private companies, groups of physicians, pharmacies or hospitals. They accept most kinds of insurance, but usually you do not need insurance to get medical care there. For some of these clinics, you can simply walk in without an appointment.
- Some issues may be addressed at a pharmacy-based walk clinic. Find these at **www. healthcare311.com**

Types of Medical Professionals

family practitioner: a physician with a specialization in general medicine for adults and children

pediatrician: a physician with a specialization in pediatrics or health care for children

internist: a physician with a specialization in internal medicine or health care for adults

registered nurse: a graduate of a four-year university with a specialization in nursing

licensed practical nurse: a graduate of a post-high-school training program in nursing

nurse practitioner: a registered nurse with graduate training who is allowed to diagnose and prescribe medicine

physician's assistant: a person with graduate training who is allowed, while working with a doctor, to diagnose and prescribe medicine; usually not a registered nurse

dentist: a graduate of dental school, usually in general dental practice

dental hygienist: a dental assistant who cleans teeth

Health Insurance Vocabulary

Managed care: This is a system of providing health care in which you cannot go to see a specialist without the approval of your primary care physician (see below); most health plans today provide managed care

Health maintenance organization (HMO): This is a group of doctors (including specialists) who work in a single organization (and, usually, a single building); members have a primary care physician who manages their care

Point of service (POS) plan: This plan is like an HMO, except members can see a specialist who is not part of the group, without a referral from their primary care physician; the POS will pay all or (more commonly) part of the specialist's fee

Preferred provider organization (PPO): In this plan groups of doctors (including specialists) agree to provide care to members at a discounted fee; members must choose a doctor from the group; doctors' offices may be anywhere in the city, and may not be in one building

Pediatricians for Children

Many pediatricians have hours during the day for parents to call in with questions. These hours are usually early in the morning. Your doctor may rely on you to say how ill your child seems. This is a good time to be very direct and open. If you are worried, ask for an appointment to see the doctor. This call-in period is also very useful for non-emergency medical or parental advice.

Hospitals

If your doctor tells you to go to a hospital, he/she will discuss with you which hospital to choose.

Medications

If you need a medicine that requires a doctor's prescription, you must go to a drug store (pharmacy) that has a registered pharmacist on staff. For most prescriptions the order can be sent to the pharmacy electronically. Your doctor will know which prescriptions can go to pharmacy electronically and which (usually controlled substances, like some stimulants, pain relievers and sedatives) require a paper prescription which you must handcarry to the drug store. For drugs that require a paper prescription for the initial prescription and all refills you will have to show a photo ID when you pickup your medicine.

Unless your doctor specifically asks for a particular brand of drug, the pharmacist will give you the least expensive generic brand for the medicine you need (generic brands are less expensive but chemically the same as other types). Filling a prescription typically takes around 15 minutes or longer. You can drop off a prescription and return later to pick it up. Or, your doctor may be able to call the prescription into your pharmacy.

Other medicines can be bought over-the-counter (without a doctor's prescription). Over-the-counter medicines are usually weaker than prescription medicines. You can buy many over-the-counter medicines at a pharmacy, a supermarket, or discount department store. Many large drug stores also make their own brands of these medicines. They are chemically the same and usually less expensive. Compare the "Active Ingredients" of the two brands. However, if you have questions about what medicine to use, or what would be similar to drugs you took at home, ask a pharmacist, who will help you choose the right medication. There is a wide selection of medications for almost every medical condition. See the Box in this chapter for the names of some common ones.

Pharmacies

You will find pharmacies in nearly every chain drug store (like CVS, Walgreens, or Rite Aid), usually near the back of the store, as well as in most large supermarkets (like Stop & Shop or Shaws). Some pharmacies offer home delivery and a way for you to order refills by telephone. If you order from an on-line pharmacy, be sure it has been approved by the National Association of Boards of Pharmacy (**www.safe.pharmacy/ buying-safely/#USPharmacies**).

Emergencies

If you need medical care very quickly, go to the Emergency Room of the closest hospital. Look online or in the Yellow Pages under Hospital to find the address of the nearest hospital Emergency Room, and learn how to get there quickly.

Indemnity policy: Not very common today, this health care policy allows you to see any doctor without any referral.

Primary care physician: This is the doctor who is assigned to manage your care; this will be the doctor you usually see when you have any illness — pediatricians for children and internists, family practitioners, or general practitioners for adults

Co-payment: You must pay this amount of money when you see a doctor, even if you have insurance

Deductible: You pay for a set amount of medical costs at the first of the year. After which the insurance company pays (perhaps with a co-payment). This is your deductible.

In most towns in Massachusetts, you can dial "911" on your telephone to reach help for any kind of emergency — medical, fire, or crime. Teach this number to your children, and tape it next to all the telephones in your home. Use it only in a serious emergency.

Popular Over-the-Counter Medications

Please read the directions and/or talk with a pharmacist before using any over-the-counter medications, especially for children and especially if you are taking any other medication or have any other diseases. Many brands of drugs have special products for children and infants. Read the labels carefully. Many cold medicines include several of these drugs — read the labels to find out what is in each multi-symptom medication. Or buy single-drug products only, so you take only the medicine you need. Also keep in mind that you may be asked to show identification to prove that you are over 18 years of age when purchasing some cough and cold medicines.

Problem	Sample Brand Names	Generic Name
Headache or Fever	Bayer, Bufferin Tylenol, Tempra Advil, Motrin Aleve	aspirin acetaminophen ibuprofen naproxen sodium
Allergy, Sneezing, Runny Nose	Benedryl ChlorTrimeton Tavist-1 Claritin	diphenhydramine hydrochloride chlorpheniramine maleate clemastine fumarate loratadine
Cough (calms)	Robitussin Maximum	*dextromethorphan hydrobromide
Stuffy Nose	Sudafed, Triaminic Afrin nasal spray	**pseudoephedrine phenylephrine hydrochloride
Stomach acid	Mylanta, Maalox Tums	aluminum, magnesium, and simethicone calcium carbonate
Diarrhea	Imodium Diasorb Pepto-Bismol	loperamide attapulgite bismuth subsalicylate
Constipation	Milk of Magnesia	magnesium hydroxide
Insect Bites	Benedryl Calamine lotion	diphenhydramine calamine

*   Some pharmacies require an ID.
**Must request from pharmacy staff.

Notes

If You Have Children

Public Schools

In most communities in the Boston area children attend school in their neighborhood, unless a bilingual program is available at another school in the system.

However, in the city of **Boston**, parents can state their preferences about which school their child will attend. Registration procedures are clearly described at **www.bostonpublicschools.org** (click on "Enroll" then "School Registration"). Information is available in nine languages.

The city of **Cambridge** uses a Controlled Choice Plan to assign children to its schools. Parents can name up to three choices of school; these choices are used along with demographic factors as part of the student assignment process. See **www.cpsd.us/departments/frc/making_your_choices/about_controlled_choice.**

Schools

If you have school-age children, finding the best school for them will be one of the most important considerations when you look for a home. You may have a choice among:

- an international private school
- an American private school
- a school run by a religious group like the Catholic Church
- a public school

Comparing Schools

Public schools may be "free" to you, depending on your visa status. But remember that you will be paying for them indirectly (through property taxes or rent) whether or not your children go there. Public schools must admit any child living in the community. Private and church-run schools charge you a tuition fee. The most expensive ones are not necessarily the best for your child.

About 85% of the children in Massachusetts go to public schools. There is a big range in the methods used in schools in the US. Ask your co-workers or relocation professional for recommendations about schools. Just remember that a school's reputation (as "good" or "bad") may be out of date or based on factors that are not relevant to you.

For detailed information about a town's school system, go to the Massachusetts Department of Education's site (**profiles.doe.mass.edu/**). You can compare school districts and schools within districts on finances, student and teacher characteristics and much more.

Registration

To register for a public school, you will have to show that you live in that community. Bring your lease, purchase and sales agreement, or a utility bill that shows your name and address. Bring your child's passport too, to show his or her birthdate. If possible, bring school records and work samples from the past two years, so the school can place your child in the most appropriate class.

Common Public School System Structures

grade				age	curriculum
12	Senior High School	Senior High School	Senior High School	17	continue academic preparation; business and technical courses
11				16	
10				15	
9	Junior High School			14	students have some choices; begin foreign languages; begin academic specialization
8				13	
7		Elementary (Primary) School	Middle School	12	
6	Elementary (Primary) School			11	
5			Elementary (Primary) School	10	reading, math, science, social studies, music, art, all subjects required for all students
4				9	
3				8	
2				7	
1				6	
K	kindergarten (not required)			5	pre-academics
PS	pre-school or nursery school (not required)			3,4	social skills and play

Understanding American Schools

Learn much more about US schools by reading *Understanding American School* by Dr. Anne Copeland (a co-author of this book) and Georgia Bennett, available at: **www.interchangeinstitute.org/html/schools.htm**

Medical Records and Immunization Requirements

Also talk to your children's school about what medical records you will need to register your child. Children entering kindergarten must have a lead screening test because lead has been found to cause learning problems in young children.

Children entering any preschool, school, or college will also have to provide a record of their immunizations. Depending on their age, they may have to have had immunizations against hepatitis B, diphtheria, tetanus, pertussis (whooping cough), Haemophilus influenzae b (Hib), polio, measles, mumps, rubella, chicken pox (varicella) and/or meningococcal disease. Massachusetts requirements change from year to year, so be sure to check for the current regulations by going to **www.mass.gov/eohhs/docs/dph/cdc/immunization/guidelines-ma-school-requirements.pdf**.

Bring a record of your children's immunizations when you register them for school. Otherwise, you must arrange for these shots to be given before starting school. Your Massachusetts pediatrician or clinic will tell you how to have your child immunized safely to meet the state requirements. See the chapter on Medical Concerns for suggestions about how to get these shots if you do not already have a doctor. Or call your child's school nurse or the Massachusetts Department of Public Health, (617) 624-6000 or go to **www.mass.gov/dph** with questions.

Finding Activities for Your Child

Being a parent in a foreign country may seem lonely until you get involved with the city and other families. Luckily, Boston has many wonderful resources for families with children of all ages.

Many public schools have after-school programs for children with working parents. They usually operate from the end of the school until 5 or 6 pm and cost a small fee. The children usually play in the school's playground or gym, have a snack, do homework, and participate in extracurricular activities like science club or music class.

A good place to meet people with small children is your public library (see the government pages of your telephone book to find the closest one — libraries are run by town governments). Go to the children's section where many libraries have toys, blocks, and puppets, as well as books. These rooms are especially good during rainy days. You may read books to your child or let him/her play under your supervision. This is a safe place to start conversations with children and other adults. Many public libraries also offer story hours and singing hours for young children. The librarian will be able to help you find other places in your town to go with your child.

Another wonderful place to meet mothers, fathers, baby-sitters or grandparents is at the playground. Bring some toys, buckets, shovels, trucks, and balls. You will soon attract other children and their caregivers. If you bring two shovels, two balls, or two trucks, sharing is easier for your child. You will have a peaceful play time and an easy first contact with other adults. Watch and listen for a while, then if you feel comfort-

When you visit a school

- Ask for a meeting with someone who can answer your questions. For public schools, call the Principal's Office or Guidance Office. For private schools, call the Admissions Office.

- Ask about the size of classes. Do teachers have helpers? What programs do they have for children who need extra help or extra challenge?

- Try to understand how the school philosophy differs from what you have at home. It will surely be different. The question is "can your child benefit from being here?"

- Look at the school building and grounds, as an outer sign of the financial status of the school.

- Ask about other international children in the school. If there are no (or very few) children from your culture in the school, your child may feel isolated. But if there are many children from your culture, your child may be slower to learn English and to make American friends.

- Ask about language help. Is there a bilingual program, or a class in English as a foreign language?

Be sure to have all your questions answered.

7 Tips to Help Your Child Learn English

1 - Continue to speak your native language and read to your children in your native language, even if you are strongly committed to learning English. Children will more easily learn a second language if they are strong in a first.

2 - At the same time, be a role model for learning English for your children. By speaking English some of the time, you will be showing your children that you think learning English is a good thing to do, and that making mistakes is OK.

3 - Look for ways your child can practice English with one or two other people. It feels less risky to speak English to one person than to a group.

4 - Understand that children often have a "silent period" when they first try English — a time when they will not speak English. This may last quite a while, although it usually doesn't. Be patient. Your child is learning to understand English, even if she/he is not speaking it.

able, start talking. This is often the best place to learn about your new neighborhood — where to buy good shoes, where to swim, or what laundry detergent is best.

Here are some other sources:

- The Boston Parents' Paper provides many ideas for classes, summer camps, entertainment, schools, special events, where to buy children's clothes or furniture, etc. Call (617) 522-1515 or go to **bostonparentspaper.com**.
- Freedman Center for Child & Family Development is an organization that connects parents to each other. Call (617) 332-3666 or go to **www.williamjames.edu/community/ freedman-center** for up-to-date information.
- Many towns provide classes for toddlers in public schools. You will probably have to pay for these, but they are usually inexpensive. Call your City/Town Hall for information, or look on the town website.
- Some health clubs provide child care. This is a wonderful way to give yourself a break and have your child socialize with others. Search on line for 'Exercise and Physical Fitness Programs' and your town's name.
- The Young Men's Christian Association (YMCA, or sometimes just called "The Y") and the Young Women's Christian Association (YWCA) offer sports activities for adults and children at a reasonable fee. Many clubs have a swimming pool. You do not have to be Christian or any particular sex to go to either the YMCA or the YWCA. Call the Boston Central (Huntington Avenue) Office at (617) 536-7800; or go to **www.ymcaboston.org** and use your zip code to search for the facility nearest you.

- There are many gymnastics centers and sports clubs in the area; most of these offer classes for babies through adolescents. Use the internet to search for Gymnastics Instruction in the Boston area.
- Go to **www.mass.gov/eea/agencies/dcr/massparks** for a good list of family, nature, and sports activities.

Child Care

If you need someone to watch your children on a regular basis during the day, you will want to consider one of several day care options. The group-based types should all be licensed by the state of Massachusetts, which regulates the adult:child ratio, the training of the staff, and health and safety issues. There are several categories of child care:

- **day care center** — a group of children (infants, toddlers, and/or pre-schoolers) with licensed adults, usually held in some non-home building (like a school, church, or apartment building); usually has long daytime hours to meet the needs of working parents
- **nursery school or pre-school** — also a group of children (age 2 years 9 months to 5 years) with licensed teachers; often half-days or only several days per week
- **family child care** — a group of children in the caregiver's home; state license requirements allow up to six children or more, depending on the age of the children; in larger groups, a licensed assistant must also be present
- **nanny or au pair** — one person caring for your child in your home; nannies are usually

5 - Remember that young children who are learning two languages at once are processing both languages, and may appear to be slower at speaking and reading than their friends. Don't panic. They are doing something more difficult. The reward will be knowing two languages.

6 - Realize that it takes up to seven years to learn a language well. Your child may be speaking English competently within six months or a year, but to function fully in school (or for you, in your adult life), it takes much longer.

7 - Understand that there is an emotional aspect to learning a second language. If learning English has a positive tone to it (for example, if your child wants to learn, she thinks her parents are happy about learning English, and English has pleasant associations to it) learning will be faster. Do not pressure your child or be critical of how quickly he or she is learning English.

Activities with Children

Boston Public Garden
Beacon Hill
(617) 723-8144; ride Swan
Boats in warm weather; ice
skate in winter
friendsofthepublicgarden.org/our-parks/public-garden/

Franklin Park Zoo
1 Franklin Park Rd., Boston
(617) 541-5466
www.zoonewengland.org/franklin-park-zoo

Stone Zoo
149 Pond Street, Stoneham
(617) 541-5466; live, not
stone animals
www.zoonewengland.org/stonezoo

Arnold Arboretum
125 Arborway, Jamaica
Plain
(617) 524-1718; 265 acres
of woodland and park
www.arboretum.harvard.edu

Blue Hills Trailside Museum
1904 Canton Avenue,
Milton
(617) 333-0690; hiking, live
animal museum
www.massaudubon.org/bluehills

Boston Children's Theatre
41 Berkeley St., Boston
527 Tremont St. Boston
545 Cabot St. Beverly
(617) 424-6634; live the-
ater for children by children
www.bostonchildrenstheatre.org

Childrens Museum
308 Congress Street,
Boston
(617) 426-6500
www.bostonchildrensmuseum.org/

professional child-care workers; au pairs are usually from other countries who are in the US primarily for the cultural experience

Each of these options has advantages and dis-advantages. US research has shown that no one of these options is best — you must look for high quality in the type you choose. Consider:

- the adult:child ratio,
- the training, patience, education, and disci-pline style of the adults,
- how often your child will get individual attention,
- the cleanliness and safety of the space,
- whether your goals for social play with other children, learning, and/or independence will be met, and
- what will happen in case of illness.

For help in finding child care in your area, call:

Child Care Choices of Boston (for Boston, Brookline, Cambridge, Chelsea, Revere, Somer-ville and Winthrop)
105 Chauncy Street, 2nd Fl.
Boston, MA 02111
(617) 542-5437
www.childcarechoicesofboston.org

Or call the Department of Early Education and Care (EEC), (617) 988-6600, or check their web site at **www.mass.gov/edu/birth-grade-12/ early-education-and-care/find-early-educa-tion-and-care-programs/**. Put in your zipcode and it will list the names and telephone numbers of licensed family and day care centers near you.

If you have an unexpected child care need, ask your employer if it provides access to emergency child care services, like Parents in a Pinch (**www.parentsinapinch.com**), a Brookline-based service.

Drumlin Farm Wildlife Sanctuary
208 South Great Road, Lincoln
(781) 259-2200; demonstration farm with animals, crops
www.massaudubon.org/drumlin

Wheelock Family Theatre
200 The Riverway, Boston
(617) 879-2300; plays for children age 3 to teens
www.wheelockfamilytheatre.org

Puppet Showplace Theatre
32 Station Street, Brookline
(617) 731-6400; puppet shows for ages 3 +
www.puppetshowplace.org

Tougas Family Farm
234 Ball Street, Northborough
(508) 393-6406; pick fruit, pet animals
www.tougasfamilyfarm.com

Great Brook Farm State Park
165 North Rd., Carlisle
(978) 369-6312; walk, see farm animals, ducks
www.mass.gov/eea/agencies/
dcr/massparks/region-north/great-brook-farm-state.html

New England Aquarium
1 Central Wharf, Boston
(617) 973-5200;
www.neaq.org

Six Flags New England
1623 Main Street, Agawam
(413) 786-9300; amusement park
www.sixflags.com/newengland

Notes

Exploring Boston

Massachusetts at a Glance

Official Name:
Commonwealth of Massachusetts
Population: 6,900,000
State Capital:
Boston population: 690,000
Greater Boston area:
4,800,000
Area:
8,257 square miles
(21,386 square km)
Communities:
302 towns; 49 cities
Elected Officers:
Governor, Lieutenant Governor, Secretary of the Commonwealth, Attorney General, Treasurer, and Auditor (elected for four years)
Legislature:
House of Representatives: 160 Members
Senate: 40 Members
(elected for 2 years)
Average temp:
January 28.2ºF,
July 72.0ºF
State Tree: American Elm
State Flower: Mayflower
State Song:
All Hail to Massachusetts
by Arthur Marsh
State Motto:
Ense petit placidam sub libertate quietem
(By the sword we seek peace, but, peace only under liberty)

For More Information:
www.mass.gov/portal/

Massachusetts History

The first humans to live in North America walked here, from what is now China and Russia, over 12,000 years ago. These groups settled in different parts of North and South America, developing their own languages, societies, and religions. The group of Native Americans who met the 16th- and 17th-century Europeans in what is now Massachusetts were called the Wampanoags. These Native Americans saved the lives of these European settlers by bringing them food and teaching them how to live in this climate. War and disease eventually destroyed much of the Native American culture in the United States. Today, Wampanoags still live in the Mashpee area.

Explorers and settlers came to different parts of the "New World" to expand the empires of England, France, Spain, Russia, and The Netherlands. English settlers were the earliest to move to the Massachusetts area — in fact, this part of the US (ME, VT, NH, MA, RI, CT) is still called "New England." Today, you can go to a re-creation of the first English settlement and a Native American home, at Plimoth Plantation (see the list of historic sites on page 111).

By the middle of the 1700s, England had gained control of all 13 North American colonies along the east coast. But gaining this control had cost a lot of money. Colonists had to pay a series of taxes to England. The colonists thought these taxes were unfair. The colonists also thought that the English Parliament did not represent their interests very well. These disagreements led to the American Revolutionary War. Many Revolutionary War events took place in Mass.

In 1770, for example, British soldiers shot guns into a crowd of citizens, killing four and wounding eight. This "Boston Massacre" angered the colonists. Then in 1773, a group of colonists decided to show their feelings about a tax on tea. They threw 342 chests of tea (worth £10,000) from a British ship into the Boston harbor rather than pay the tax, in what is called the "Boston Tea Party."

In 1775, British soldiers in Massachusetts marched from Lexington to Concord to take the colonists' weapons away from them. William

---

Historical Sites

Freedom Trail: a walking tour of historic Boston; follow the red lines painted on the sidewalk
from Visitor Center;139 Tremont Street Boston, 2.5 miles, 16 sites; (617) 357-8300 to reserve place in guided tour, or go by yourself. Tours start at 148 Tremont Street.
www.thefreedomtrail.org

Black Heritage Trail: a walking tour of African American history
from Visitor Center; 46 Joy Street, Boston, 1.6 miles, 14 sites; (617) 742-5415 to reserve place in guided tour, or go by yourself
www.afroammuseum.org/trail.htm

Boston Tea Party Ship & Museum: replica of ship where Boston Tea Party happened
306 Congress Street Bridge, Boston, (866) 955-0667
www.bostonteapartyship.com

USS Constitution: oldest commissioned ship in the US Navy
Building 22, Charlestown Navy Yard; (617) 426-1812
www.ussconstitutionmuseum.org

Old North Bridge: site of the first battle of the American Revolution
174 Liberty St., Concord
www.nps.gov/mima/index.htm

Plimoth Plantation: re-creation of the Pilgrims' town, ship, and an Indian homesite
137 Warren Ave., Plymouth, MA, (508) 746-1622
www.plimoth.org

Old Sturbridge Village: 40 buildings from 1790-1840 re-create a New England town
1 Old Sturbridge Village Rd. (exit 9 of the Mass. Turnpike), Sturbridge, MA; (800) 733-1830
www.osv.org

Witch Museum: site of witch trials of 17th century
19½ Washington Square, North Salem, MA; (978) 744-1692
www.salemwitchmuseum.com

Also see **www.masshome.com/hist.html** for more information about Massachusetts historical sites and societies.

Popular Museums

Note: Holders of a Metro Boston Library Network card may be able to borrow a one-day museum pass (for free family admission) for some of these museums. Reserve on line at www.bpl.org/general/circulation/museum_passes.php#whomay

Museum of Fine Arts
465 Huntington Ave., Boston, (617) 267-9300; www.mfa.org
M, Tu: 10-5; W, Th, F: 10-10; Sa, Su: 10-5

Institute of Contemporary Art
100 Northern Avenue., Boston, (617) 478-3100 www.icaboston.org
T, W: 10-5; Th, F 10-9; Sa, Su; 10-5; closed M and closed 5pm first F of each month

Isabella Stewart Gardner Museum
280 The Fenway, Boston; (617) 566-1401 www.gardnermuseum.org
11-5 except Th: 11-9 and closed Tu

New England Aquarium
Central Wharf, Boston; (617) 973-5200; www.neaq.org
M-F: 9-5; Sa & Su and some holidays 9-6; open one hour later during summer

Museum of Science
Science Park, Boston; (617) 723-2500; www.mos.org
M-Su: 9-5 except F 9-9;

Children's Museum
300 Congress St., Boston, (617) 426-6500 www.bostonchildrensmuseum.org
M-Su: 10-5 except F 10-9;

John F. Kennedy Library
Columbia Point, Boston 02125-3398; (617) 514-1600 www.jfklibrary.org
Every day: 9-5 except some holidays;

Museum of Afro American History
46 Joy St., Boston; (617) 725-0022 maah.org/
M-Sa: 10-4; closed Su

Harvard and MIT Museums
both universities have several small art or science museums: www.harvardartmuseums.org or mitmuseum.mit.edu/visit

ready to fight in a minute) in Concord (at a bridge you can visit). There they fired what Americans call the "shot heard around the world" — the first shot in the American Revolutionary War. Every year this battle is re-created in Lexington and Concord, early in the morning of Patriot's Day (the third Monday of April).

Colonists signed the Declaration of Independence in 1776 in Philadelphia. Americans celebrate this signing on the Fourth of July. The Revolutionary War finally ended in 1783 with the signing of the Treaty of Paris. On February 6, 1788, Massachusetts became the sixth colony (of the original 13) to join the new United States of America.

Massachusetts' role in American history in the next 200 years was based largely on its place as an industrial center (especially of shoes and textiles), a port (shipping more than $8 billion worth of goods every year), an educational center (there are 65 colleges and universities here), a medical center (25 medical research institutions), and recently, a center of technology.

Arts Guide

Boston is the cultural and performing arts center of New England. Many of its museums are world-class. There are always many performances to choose from. Ask about student discounts. Call to get on a mailing list. See the list of Museums in this chapter. Or try the sources in the Sidebar.

Learn About Performances

Bostix: ½-price tickets on day of performance; order online (www.bostix.org), or at ticket booths at Faneuil Hall (Tu-Su 10-4) or Copley Square (Tu-F 11-5; Sa-Su10-4)

Arts Boston: tickets and information about many performances: artsboston.org

Boston Globe Calendar: lists performances in Thursday's Globe; calendar.boston.com

Movie Listings: www.moviefone.com www.fandango.com

LiveNation: tickets online for many performing arts events, www.livenation.com

TicketMaster: tickets for most performing arts and sports events, (800)-653-8000; www.ticketmaster.com

Performing Arts Centers

Boston Symphony Orchestra (BSO)
Symphony Hall, 301 Mass. Ave, Boston (Sept - April); (888) 266-1200
297 West St.,Tanglewood, Lenox, MA (July-August); (888) 266-1200
www.bso.org

Boston Pops Orchestra
Symphony Hall, 301 Mass. Ave , Boston (spring), Charles River Esplanade Hatch Shell, Boston (July) (888) 266-1200, (Hatch Shell free); www.bso.org

Handel and Haydn Society
9 Harcourt St, Boston; (617) 262-1815
www.handelandhaydn.org

American Repertory Theatre
Loeb Drama Center, 64 Brattle St., Cambridge; (617) 547-8300
americanrepertorytheater.org/

Huntington Theatre
264 Huntington Ave., Boston; (617) 266-0800
www.huntingtontheatre.org

Boch Center (Shubert Theatre and Wang Theatre)
270 Tremont St., Boston, (617) 482-9393
www.bochcenter.org

Boston Opera House
539 Washington St. Boston (617) 259-3400
www.bostonoperahouse.com

Boston Lyric Opera
Performances at Shubert Theater: 265 Tremont St, Boston. Admin. office: 11 Avenue de Lafayette, Boston
(617) 542-4912;
www.blo.org

Many colleges and universities in Boston are part of the University Membership program of the Museum of Fine Arts. These institutions pay each year for their students to have free access to the MFA's permanent collection and discounts on tickets to temporary exhibitions and Museum Shop purchases if they present a valid student ID. Check the list at **www.mfa.org/membership/universities** to see if your university is a member of this program.

Public Libraries

We recommend that you find your closest public library and explore it. It is a valuable resource for you and your children. Public libraries play an important role as a center of community information. The sponsors of any town event, concert, fair, or meeting will post a sign at the library.

You can find a list of the Boston Public Library's branches at **www.bpl.org/branches** and a list of 36 public and 7 college libraries in the Greater Boston area that are members of the Minuteman Library Network at **www.mln.lib.ma.us**.

Anyone can enter any public library and use the resources there. To take a book home, however, you will need a library card. Usually you can get a card by showing something with your name and address printed on it (like a lease or a Massachusetts driver's license). Some towns require an identification that has your picture on it. Children can get their own cards, too.

It is free to borrow books from public libraries. If you return the book late, however, you may have to pay a fine (usually a few cents per day). Fines on children's cards are often lower than those on adult cards, so have your children use their own.

Once you have a card for one library, you can take books home from libraries in some nearby towns, too. (Ask your librarian for the names of other libraries in your group.) Or your librarian may be able to order a book from another library in the group by telephone; it will be delivered to your town library within a few days, for you to pick up there. If you borrow a book from one library, you can return it to any library in the group.

Volunteering

A great way to get involved around Boston and meet the locals is to do a community service activity. There are many opportunities, including volunteer jobs for people who have busy schedules. To find a volunteer project, check one of these internet sites:

www.volunteermatch.org
www.idealist.org

These free volunteer matching websites contain lists of over a thousand ways to help people throughout Boston. Just type in your zip code and the type of social issue you are interested in.

If you have a hectic schedule and do not have the ability to commit to long-term projects, try contacting Boston Cares. This organization offers many options with small time commitments, such as food distribution at a homeless shelter or visiting with the elderly. See **www.bostoncares.org** or call (617) 422-0910.

Rush (Discount) Tickets

These tickets are available at a discounted rate on a first-come, first-serve basis.

Boston Symphony Orchestra (BSO) Rush Tickets

Discount tickets for people <40 years old. One ticket per customer. Cash only. Limited number available.

Boston Ballet Rush Tickets

Two hours before performance at the Wang Theater Box Office Window. For children 2-17, full time college students and seniors 65+. One ticket per customer. Cash only. Limited number available. Call to confirm availability (617) 695-6955.

Boston Lyric Opera Rush Tickets

Available for students 90 minutes before performance, when available. Valid Student ID required. See other discount offers at blo.org/discounts-offers/

5 Tips for Meeting People and Getting Involved

1 - Join an association or club for people interested in a **sport or activity** you enjoy. For example: Appalachian Mountain Club (hiking, biking, canoeing, and other outdoor activities): www.amcboston.org

2 - Join a club or group designed to **help people meet each other**.

3 - **Volunteer to help a cause** that is important to you. This kind of experience can build your resume, even if you are not paid for the work.

4 - Attend a meeting or event at a **cultural organization from your home country**. Ask at your Consulate (see page 86) for a list of such organizations.

5 - **Try an on-line approach to finding others with your interests**. Go to www.meetup.com and click on Boston for a list of dozens of groups that meet around common interests. Note the "Expatriates" category.

Finally, there are many community groups that do not advertise opportunities, but that welcome volunteers. If there is an organization in your neighborhood that interests you, call or visit them, and offer your services.

Sports

The Sidebar in this chapter shows the major professional spectator sports in Massachusetts. Local colleges and universities are also good places to watch sports.

Rules of Baseball

Here are some rules to help you watch your first baseball game:

- Two teams of nine players take turns being up at bat and in the field. An inning is one cycle of turns (Team A is up at bat, then Team B is up at bat). A game has 9 innings.

- A baseball field has a diamond and an outfield. The diamond is the runway connecting four corner bases: home plate, and first, second, and third bases. The outfield is the space on the outside of the diamond. The team that is in the field has one player in each position: pitcher (who throws the ball to the batter on the other team), catcher (who is behind the batter at home base), first, second, and third basemen (one at each base), short stop (who stands between second and third base), and three outfielders (who stand far back, out in left, center, and right field).

- While the batter stands beside home plate, the pitcher must throw the ball directly over home plate at a height that falls between the batter's knees and shoulders. If the ball is outside

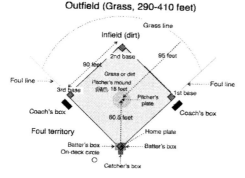

Outfield (Grass, 290-410 feet)

this target area, the batter should not swing at it; it's called a ball. If the pitcher throws four such balls to one batter, the batter gets to walk to first base without interruption. If the ball is inside the target area, the batter should swing at it. If he swings and misses, it's called a strike. If the batter does not swing at a ball that is in the target area, it's also considered a strike. If he gets three strikes in one turn, he has struck out and his turn is over. If he hits the ball in such a way that it goes high in the air, it's called a fly ball. If the other team catches a fly ball before it touches the ground, the batter is out and has to leave the field.

- If the batter hits the ball, he tries to run to each base (in order, to first base, then second, third, and home) before the other team can throw the ball there, or can touch the batter with the ball. He tries to run to as many bases as he can. Most often, he will only get to first base before the other team gets the ball there. If it is a close race, the batter stops at first base, and the next batter takes a turn. If the ball gets to the base before the batter, the batter is out and he leaves the field.

- When the next batter starts to run to first base,

Boston's Professional Sports Teams

Baseball
Boston Red Sox
Fenway Park, 4 Yawkey Way, Boston
(877) 733-7699
www.mlb.com/redsox
starts at $20; Apr.- Oct.

Basketball
Boston Celtics
TD Banknorth Garden, Causeway & Nashua Streets, Boston
(866) 423-5849
www.nba.com/celtics
Jan.-June

Football
New England Patriots
Gillette Stadium
Route 1, Foxborough
(800) 543-1776
www.patriots.com
Aug.-Jan.

Hockey
Boston Bruins
TD Banknorth Garden, Causeway & Nashua Streets, Boston
(617) 624-2327
www.nhl.com/bruins/
Oct -Apr.

Soccer
New England Revolution
Gillette Stadium
Route 1, Foxborough
(877) 438-7387
www.revolutionsoccer.net
Mar.-Oct. men's team

Sports Idioms

Now it is her turn to be up at bat.
Now it is her turn to be the leader.

It is a whole new ball game now.
Everything has changed.

She could not get to first base with her plan.
She could not make her plan work or convince any-one to be interested in it.

The book you wrote is a home run.
The book you wrote is a great success.

We need a power hitter for this project.
We need our strongest person for this project.

You were really on the ball this morning.
You were really alert and effective this morning.

I tried to make a reserva-tion at lots of restau-rants, but I have struck out.
I tried to make a reserva-tion at lots of restaurants, but I was unsuccessful.

He is out in left field.
His ideas are very unusual and different from other people's.

Let's kick off the year with a special dinner.
Let's begin the year with a special celebration dinner.

the first player runs toward second base. The player on second base runs toward third. The player on third runs to home base. A batter scores a run (a point) when he gets back to home plate. Players in the outfield try to get the ball to a base before a batter gets there. If they succeed, the batter is out.

- Sometimes, of course, the batter can get to second or third base, or even all the way around to home plate before the ball catches up with him. This is called a home run, or a homer. If a batter gets a home run when the bases are loaded (there is a player from his team on first, second, and third base when he steps up to bat), it is called a grand slam. All four batters score runs in that turn.

- When players on the team at bat have had three outs, the other team comes up to bat. The team with the most points at the end of nine innings wins.

Rules of American Football
Americans play football in elementary school, high school, college, and professionally. The rules at these levels differ slightly. They also change frequently, to keep the game safe and fair. Here are the current professional rules:

Basic Facts:
- A football is a pointed-oval shaped ball, about 11 inches long and 7 inches wide. It weighs 14-15 ounces.

- Playing time is 60 minutes (four 15-minute quarters). But the clock stops often, for vari-ous reasons (for example, after every scored point, and in case of penalties, injuries, and incomplete passes). There is a break after two quarters that may include entertainment and marching bands. Including the half-time break, a typical professional game takes 2.5 to 3 hours.

- Each team has 11 players. When a team has control of the ball and is advancing toward the other team's goal line, they are playing offense. The other team, at that moment, is playing defense. Usually, players specialize in playing offense or defense, and in one of several positions such as quarterback, halfback, fullback, center, guard, and end.

- A football field is 100 yards long, marked on both ends by a goal line. Then there is a 10-yard end zone, marked on both ends by an end line. There is a goal post on each end line. The goal post is really two upright (vertical) poles, connected by another horizontal pole (called the crossbar). The field is 53 1/3 yards wide.

- Each team defends one goal. The object of the game is to score points by getting the ball across the other team's goal line. Players can advance the ball by passing (throwing) or carrying it.

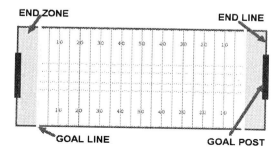

END ZONE   END LINE

GOAL LINE   GOAL POST

They are bringing out the second string now.
They are starting to use people who are not the most skillful.

That issue is a real political football.
That issue is one that people avoid because it causes so much disagreement.

Let's just run out the clock.
Let's do nothing except wait — we will be successful if we risk nothing because we are ahead now.

The ball is in your court.
I am waiting for you to act.

That's the way the ball bounces.
Luck sometimes determines an outcome.

I am willing to go to the mat about this.
I am willing to fight hard until I win.

You lost, but just roll with the punch and we'll try again tomorrow.
You lost, but don't spend time worrying about it — we'll try again tomorrow.

We are down to the wire on this project.
We will just barely finish this project by the deadline.

Talk like a Native...

Here are some tips for talking like a Boston native:

Quincy Market: It's pronounced "KWIN-zee" not "KWIN-see"

Faneuil Hall: It's pronounced "FAN-ull" not "FAN-you-ul"

Massachusetts Avenue: People call it "Mass Ave" (pronounced "Mass Av")

Commonwealth Avenue: People call it "Comm Ave" (pronounced "Cahm Av")

Tremont Street (It's pronounced TREH-mont, not TREE-mont)

Copley Square (It's pronounced COP-ly not COPE-ly)

• Teams score points in 4 ways:

touchdown (6 points): a player carries the ball over the other team's goal line, or when a player catches the ball while he is in the other team's end zone

field goal (3 points): a player kicks the ball over the crossbar of the other team's goal post

safety (2 points): a player with the ball is stopped in his own end zone, the other team gets the points and becomes the offensive team

PAT: after a team scores a touchdown, it can try a point after touchdown (PAT) play — by either kicking the ball through the goal post upright (for 1 point) or passing or carrying it across the goal line again from the 2-yard line (for 2 points)

The Game:

Each half of the game starts with a kickoff. Near the center of the field, a player from Team B kicks the ball off the ground toward Team A's goal line. Team A tries to catch the ball and run toward Team B's goal line. Team B runs toward the ball, trying to stop Team A from advancing. At this moment, Team A is playing offense, Team B defense. That play ends when any one of these happen:

• Team B tackles the Team A player who has the ball (pushes him to the ground, or until his knee touches the ground)

• The Team A player who has the ball runs out of bounds (off the field), or

• a Team A player catches the ball in the end zone and touches his knee to the ground.

Team A forms a huddle (circle) and decides on the next play. The two teams line up on the line of scrimmage (the place on the field where the play ended). Team A is still playing offense. This time, instead of a kickoff, the center from Team A hikes the ball to the quarterback (throws or hands it to him, backward under his legs).

Team A gets four downs (plays) to advance the ball 10 yards. Every time it succeeds, it gets four more downs to advance 10 more yards. If it fails, Team B becomes the offensive team.

Sometimes, if a team realizes it is unlikely to advance the 10 yards (and will soon be playing defense), it will punt (kick) the ball as far as possible. This way, the other team has further to go when it starts to play offense.

If a Team A member passes the ball to a teammate, a player from Team B may intercept the pass (catch it instead). Team B immediately becomes the offensive team, and tries to advance to Team A's goal.

If a player breaks a rule, his team gets a penalty. A penalty may mean that the ball is put further back on the field, away from the goal, before the game continues. Or the team may "lose a down." For example, if they had been taking their second chance at advancing 10 yards, with the penalty it would be considered their third down.

The team with more points at the end of the 4th quarter wins. If the two teams are tied (have the same score), they play one more 15-minute quarter. If the score is still tied, the game ends anyway, with a tied score.

"People are not that crazy about sports in my country. It's really fun to sit in Fenway Park, watch the game, and enjoy hot dogs and a coke! Oh, remember to go with someone who knows the rules."

Menu Vocabulary

Meat, Fish, & Vegetables
broiled: under direct heat
grilled: over direct heat
char-broiled: over open flame on a grill; will show grill marks
roasted: in an oven, with some fat
baked: in an oven, with little or no fat
steamed: on stove, over steam
fried: on stove, in a little fat or oil
sautéed/stir-fried: on stove, in a little fat or oil, for a short time
deep fried: in several inches of fat or oil
poached: on stove, in liquid that is not quite 100° C
boiled: on stove, in liquid that is at 100° C

Salad Dressings
Oil and vinegar: just oil and vinegar, no spices
Vinaigrette: oil and vinegar and spices
Italian: oil and vinegar and spices
Creamy Italian: oil, vinegar, spices, and cream or sour cream
French vinaigrette: may include ketchup and sugar
Roquefort: Roquefort cheese, mayonnaise, sour cream, vinegar
Blue cheese: Blue cheese, mayonnaise, sour cream, vinegar
Thousand Island: mayonnaise, ketchup, vinegar, pickles

Restaurants

Boston has many excellent restaurants. Here is some information that will help you enjoy them.

Choosing a Restaurant

To find a good restaurant, check these websites:
- **www.yelp.com/boston**
- **www.citysearch.com/listings/boston-ma-metro/restaurants.html**
- **www.zagat.com/boston**
- **www.zomato.com/boston**

Reservations

Most restaurants are happy to take reservations. You can call several weeks ahead. Make a reservation, especially if you will be going to a popular restaurant on a Friday or Saturday night, and/or will be wanting a table for more than four people. The restaurant manager may ask for your telephone number, and may call you on the day of the reservation to confirm that you are still coming. If your plans change, it is polite to call the restaurant and cancel the reservation.

Try OpenTable (**www.opentable.com**) to make free online reservations at area restaurants. The website connects to each restaurant's reservation confirmation system over the internet. When you make a reservation on the website, the restaurant's computer records and confirms it.

Some restaurants do not take reservations, or take them only for large groups; the wait may be up to an hour on weekend nights.

Charges and Tips

See our separate section on this in the *Understanding the US* chapter for information about restaurant tips (sometimes called gratuities). You may also find that a restaurant has a minimum order, especially at busy times of the day. This means that you must order a minimum amount of food or drink. Some restaurants connected to bars or nightclubs will also have a cover charge, or a fee simply to be seated. When you are paying for your meal, the waitstaff will often take your credit card away to complete the transaction. This may be a change from what is done in your country.

Bread, Water, and Ice

If the waiter brings bread to your table without your asking for it, you will not be charged for this. Many restaurants will automatically bring ice water to your table. If you are not served water, it is always fine to ask for it. This will be water from the faucet, but will be clean in virtually every part of the United States. If you prefer bottled water, with or without bubbles, order it from the waiter. There will be a charge for bottled water. Most Americans like a lot of ice in their drinks, so that is what you will usually get. It is fine to say, "May I have a soda, without any ice, please?"

Alcohol

State laws put some limits on when and where alcohol may be served; town laws may apply further limits. In Massachusetts you cannot buy an alcoholic beverage in a restaurant or bar on a Sunday until 10 a.m. Many stores do not sell alcohol until noon on Sunday (remember the religious roots of this state). Restaurants in Massachusetts must have a license from the state to serve alcoholic beverages. Some licenses allow the sale of all types of alcohol; others only allow the sale of wine and beer. The state limits the number of licenses it gives, so some newer

Eggs
scrambled: mixed then cooked in pan while stirring
sunnyside up: broken directly into pan with yolk whole, then fried
over-easy: like sunnyside up, but cooked on both sides
soft-boiled: cooked in shell in water till solid but soft
hard-boiled: cooked in shell in water till solid and firm
poached: broken into pan with water, keeping yolk whole

Drinks (alcoholic)
up: chilled but without ice
neat: not chilled, no ice
on the rocks: with ice cubes
frozen: with crushed ice
neat or straight: without added water

Coffee
regular: with cream and sugar
decaf: de-caffeinated; coffee with caffeine removed
black: without cream, milk, or sugar

Other Useful Words
salad bar: table where you can make your own lettuce salad
tossed salad: lettuce salad, may include other vegetables too
meat/egg salads: small pieces of meat (chicken, ham), fish (canned tuna), or egg, mixed with mayonnaise
chowder/ bisque: milk-based soups, often include pieces of seafood

restaurants may not have one. In some towns, no restaurant is allowed to have a license, but you may be allowed to bring your own bottle of wine. The waiter may be able to give you a corkscrew and wine glass. When you call for a reservation, ask about this. In addition, in Massachusetts you may not drink alcohol or carry it in an open container in public places (including parks).

Smoking

In 1965, 42% of American adults smoked cigarettes; now the number is about 15%. Non-smokers (and ex-smokers) have been active in restricting where smokers may smoke in public places, including restaurants. In Massachusetts and many other states, smoking in restaurants, bars, and other establishments is illegal. You will have to go outside of the building if you would like to smoke. You also may need to be a certain distance away from the entrance to the building. In Boston, smoking in public parks is prohibited.

A new trend is to smoke tobacco-free e-cigarettes: about 4% Americans *vape* daily. Rules about e-cigarette usage are changing; watch for signs and policies if you are interested.

Vegetarians

A significant number of Americans are vegetarians, on religious, ethical, or nutritional grounds. There is quite a range in how strictly they observe a vegetarian diet — from "not eating much red meat" to vegans, who eat no meat and no animal products (like milk or eggs) at all.

There are many vegetarian restaurants in Boston. Even if you are a strict vegetarian, you should be able to find restaurant meals that have no meat

"The sign in a restaurant said, 'Please Wait to Be Seated.' It took me a long time to learn that I was supposed to wait by the sign for the restaurant hostess to tell me where to sit."

in them. However, you might want to ask the waiter questions like these:

- Does this dish contain any fish or meat in it?
- Was this soup made with a meat broth?
- Was any animal fat used in making this dish?

If the waiter is unsure, ask him to ask the chef.

Some foods may sound as if they have meat in them, like "barbecue chips," but may not.

Lobster

There are many ways to enjoy this New England classic shellfish. If you want to sit by the water and enjoy your lobster, you can go to the waterfront area, along Boston's wharf or in any seacoast town in the area. If you prefer an economical lobster meal, some supermarkets sell live lobsters and will cook them for you. Choose your own lobster, wait for 15 minutes, go home and enjoy it!

Food trucks

Many public locations in Boston have food trucks which provide a wide variety of food, ranging from crepes and lobsters to cupcakes and tacos. Check out **roaminghunger.com/bos** or **hubfoodtrucks.com.**

How to Eat a Lobster

Now that your lobster is there on the plate, what do you do? Some tips:

- Most of the meat is in the tail and claws. Some people like to get smaller bits from the legs and body, too. However, do not eat the stomach or digestive tract.

- Break off the tail by bending it backwards towards the head. Push the meat out of the shell. You may see some green substance (the digestive gland, called tomalley) and orange eggs. Some people consider these delicious.

- Twist off the claws from the main part of the lobster body.

- Use lobster (or nut) crackers to crack the claws. Push meat out of the pointed parts. The meat in the two pincer claws is the tenderest.

- Dip in melted butter with lemon.

- Enjoy!

Notes

Understanding
the US

Finding a Place to Worship

www.yellowpages.com/
boston-ma/churches-places-
of-worship

pluralism.org/profiles
  (Harvard University's Plural-
  ism Project — overview
  of many religious faiths
  in Boston, with links to
  many churches, temples,
  mosques, centers, and
  congregations.)

Religion in the US

Many newcomers to the United States are surprised by the close connection many families have to their religion. About 70% of Americans are members of a church or synagogue; about 36% go to weekly religious services. About one third of all financial donations in the US are to religious organizations.

Many people enjoy their places of worship for the friendship they find there. In the US, many families move to new homes, or even a new state, quite often. Churches and synagogues may be places where they can make new friends and enjoy activities with people who have the same values. Activities there may have a social focus. There may be trips, sports, games and dances. Activities may be for one age group or every age. There may be groups for young married couples, or for single adults.

Other activities focus on social service. They may cook and serve meals for those without homes, or bring supplies to shelters for women and children. They may hold money-raising events to support their charity activities. Other activities may focus on political or social issues.

If you are interested in American religion, feel free to go to a weekly service in your community (times are usually posted outside the churches and synagogues). If the customs are unfamiliar to you, just sit in the back and watch respectfully.

Social Issues

Tipping

Tipping is very common in the US. You may find it to be an odd practice. You should realize that because tipping is so common, the people who are tipped usually get a smaller salary. They (and their employers) consider their tips to be part of their income. Not tipping hurts the worker, not the employer.

If you think the service was poor, you do not have to tip. (Of course, if you go back to that place and they remember you, they may give you even worse service!) In the Sidebar in this Chapter, we give some suggestions about whom to tip, and how much to give. How much to give depends on how long you have known them, the number of other gifts they are likely to get, the size of your weekly payment to them, how good a job they have done, and their (and your) personal financial situation. You might give the newspaper and mail carriers $5-10 and a house cleaner or baby sitter an extra one or one-half week's pay. These numbers are estimates only. Tipping (and salaries) vary widely from town to town. It is best to ask a friend or co-worker what is typical in your area.

One note about restaurant tipping. If your group has eight or more people in it, some restaurants add 15-20% tip to your bill. In that case, you do not have to add any more tip, unless the service was outstanding. There will be a notice on the menu about this added tip for large groups if that is the restaurant's policy. Or, ask your server.

"We seldom give tips to waiters in our country. One time, my friend and I forgot to give a tip when we left the restaurant. The waiter came out after us and asked us for a tip!"

Common Tip Amounts

Restaurant/Bar
serving food: 15-20%
bartending: $1 or $2 per drink
coffee bar: 15-20% or $1 per drink

Hotel
getting taxi for you: $1
carrying your suitcase: $1-2 per bag
cleaning your room: $1-2 per day

Theater
checking your coat: $1 per coat

Airport
carrying your suitcase: $1-2 per bag

Beauty Salon
cutting hair (except owner of shop is not tipped): 15%
helping stylist, washing hair: $2-3
manicure: 10%

Barber Shop
cutting hair: 15%

Parking Lot or Car Wash
parking and bringing car to you: $2-5

Taxicab
driving: 15%

Flower or Food/Pizza Delivery
delivery to your home: 15% or $5

Invitations to a friend's home

In the United States it is common to say, "Let's get together for lunch or dinner" or "Why don't you come over some time?" These are expressions of friendliness, but are not actually invitations. When the invitation is genuine, the person will continue to plan with you, suggesting a specific date and time.

When the invitation is a written one, it is polite to respond quickly. Often the invitation will say "RSVP" (Répondez, s'il vous plaît, French for Respond, please). In that case, a reply is required, whether you will be able to go or not. Or, it may say "Regrets Only." Then, you should call only if you will not be able to attend. If a telephone number is included, you may call to reply. Email replies are OK too, for less formal invitations. And a note by mail is always OK.

If a business colleague invites you to his or her home for dinner, your spouse may be invited too. If your children are included, your host will make that clear. If you are not sure, ask the host because it is awkward to be wrong.

If you are invited to someone's home for dinner, a host or hostess gift is customary. This gift may be a bottle of wine, carried to the home, unwrapped and presented after the greeting. Do not expect the wine to be served that evening. That decision is left to the host or hostess. Other common gifts are flowers or a box of candy.

A phone call or email (for less formal events) or a short note (for more formal ones) to the hosts after the dinner is appropriate to thank them for the enjoyable evening, company and good food.

Invitations to your home

You can expect the same behavior as above when you invite someone to your home. If the person is a friend or business colleague and lives within driving distance, invite the spouse also. You do not have to invite their children, especially if you do not have children of the same age. If you would like to include the whole family, be clear that the dinner will be less formal (for example, a barbecue or a picnic at a nearby park). In that case, have some games or activities planned.

Invitations to a business dinner

Invitations to a business dinner vary from the social dinner in some very important ways. Often, business dinners are at a restaurant, not a home. Business dinners usually do not include spouses (and never include children). Most of the conversation will be about business, being part of the team, strategic planning, etc. If your spouse is invited to a dinner with your colleagues, others will bring their spouses also. Business conversation will be limited and general. The purpose of the gathering will be to strengthen relationships and the sense of group.

The person who organized the dinner usually expects to pay the bill. However, if it is a dinner of business colleagues from the same company, each person may be expected to pay for his or her own dinner. You'll know when the check arrives. If you want to be the one to pay the bill, talk to the server before the bill is brought to the table.

People Who Get a Yearly Tip or Gift

- mail carrier
- newspaper carrier
- house cleaner
- gardener
- doorman at your apartment house
- regular nanny or baby sitter

People You Should Not Tip

- airline employees
- workers in fast food restaurants
- hotel desk clerks
- teachers
- bus drivers (except airport van drivers who are tipped for baggage handling)
- gas station attendants
- store clerks
- person who carries your groceries to your car
- receptionists
- business lobby directors
- ushers in concerts, theaters, sporting events or movie houses

Note: To tip any government employees, including customs officials, fire fighters, police officers, or postal workers may be considered a bribe and is illegal.

Holidays

Because each state can choose which holidays to observe, there are technically no "national" holidays in the US. However, most states, including Massachusetts, observe most of the "federal" holidays (for employees of the US government). On these holidays, schools, government offices, banks, and many businesses will be closed. Other holidays are observed only informally. Be sure to learn which holidays will be observed by your company and schools. The chart that follows gives an explanation for many of the holidays celebrated in Massachusetts.

Holiday	Date	Meaning	Form of Observation	Business & School Closings
New Year's Day	January 1	reflect on new and past year	open house parties, watch American football on TV	schools, government, and most businesses closed
Martin Luther King, Jr. Birthday	third Monday of January	birthday of civil rights leader	discuss race issues	schools and government closed; some businesses open
Valentine's Day	February 14	show love and affection	send cards, flowers, or candy to loved ones	no closings
President's Day	third Monday in February	honor US presidents, especially Washington and Lincoln	few traditions	schools and government closed; some businesses open
St. Patrick's Day	March 17	honor the patron saint of Ireland and Irish culture	wear green, parades	Boston and some surrounding cities
Passover	14th day of Nisan, Jewish calendar	Jewish festival of freedom, celebrating the escape of the Israelites from Egypt	traditional meal, attend religious services, eat only unleavened food	some schools closed
Good Friday	Friday before Easter Sunday	Christian commemoration of the crucifixion of Jesus	attend religious services	some schools and businesses closed

Holiday	Date	Meaning	Form of Observation	Business & School Closings
Easter	first Sunday after first full moon after vernal equinox	Christian celebration of the rebirth of Jesus	attend religious services, dye and hunt for hidden Easter eggs	always a Sunday so many businesses and schools are closed
Patriot's Day	third Monday in April	beginning of the American Revolution	re-enactment of battles at dawn in Lexington, MA	schools and government closed; some businesses open
Mother's Day	2nd Sunday of May	honor mothers, both living and dead	send flowers, card, gift, visit, or telephone call	no closings
Memorial Day	last Monday of May	honor those who died while fighting in a war	parades, decorating graves of soldiers and other loved ones	schools and government closed; some businesses open
Father's Day	third Sunday in June	honor fathers, both living and dead	send card, gift, visit, or telephone call	no closings
Fourth of July	July 4	commemorate the adoption of the Declaration of Independence from England, 1776	family picnics, fireworks at night, concert on Boston Esplanade	government closed; some businesses open
Labor Day	first Monday of September	honor the laborers of the US	family picnics, marks the informal end of summer	schools and government closed
Rosh Hashanah	first day of Tishri, in Jewish calendar	Jewish New Year	symbolic family dinner, attend religious services	some schools closed
Yom Kippur	10 days after Rosh Hashanah	Jewish Day of Atonement	pray and fast, to be forgiven for sins of the past year	some schools closed
Columbus Day	second Monday in October	commemorate the landing in the New World, of Columbus in 1492	few traditions	schools and government closed; some businesses open
Halloween	October 31	old pagan harvest roots, but now a light, fun children's holiday	children dress in costume and go from neighbor to neighbor asking for candy	no closings

Holiday	Date	Meaning	Form of Observation	Business & School Closings
Veteran's Day	November 11	honor all veterans of armed forces, and the end of World War I	parades, wear red poppies	schools and government closed; some businesses open
Thanksgiving	4th Thursday of November	commemorate the first harvest of the first English settlers in 1621	big family dinner of turkey, cranberries, and pumpkin pie	schools, government, and most businesses closed (may be closed the next Friday also)
Hanukkah	25th day of Kislev, in Jewish calendar	Jewish festival of lights, to commemorate the return of the temple to Jews	light candles every night for 8 nights; children get small gifts	no closings
Christmas	December 25	Christian celebration of the birth of Jesus	family gathering, gift-giving	schools, government, and most businesses closed
Kwanzaa	December 26-January 1	celebration of African-American culture	family gathering, candle lighting to celebrate values	no closings
New Year's Eve	December 31	celebrate the end of the year	parties at midnight	closings common after 12 noon

Appendices

USEFUL BUSINESSES IN BOSTON
Visit website for locations

BANKS
Bank of America
www.bankofamerica.com
Century Bank
www.centurybank.com
Citizens Bank
www.citizensbank.com
Santander Bank
www.santanderbank.com
Capital One Bank
www.capitalone.com

SUPERMARKETS
Roche Brothers
www.rochebros.com
Shaws
www.shaws.com
Stop & Shop
www.stopandshop.com
Trader Joe's
www.traderjoes.com
Whole Foods
www.wholefoodsmarket.com
Market Basket
www.mydemoulas.net/loca-tions/massachusetts/

DISCOUNT CLOTHING
Marshalls
www.marshallsonline.com
TJ Maxx
www.tjmaxx.com

HOUSEWARES
Bed Bath and Beyond
www.bedbathandbeyond.com
Economy/True Value Hardware
www.truevalue.com
Home Depot
www.homedepot.com
Target
www.target.com
Wal-Mart
www.walmart.com

DEPARTMENT STORES
Bloomingdale's
www.bloomingdales.com
JCPenney
www.jcpenney.com
Lord and Taylor
www.lordandtaylor.com
Macy's
www.macys.com
Neiman Marcus
www.neimanmarcus.com
Saks Fifth Avenue
www.saksfifthavenue.com
Sears
www.sears.com

OFFICE SUPPLIES
Staples
www.staples.com
Office Depot
www.officedepot.com

ELECTRONICS
Best Buy
www.bestbuy.com
Radio Shack
www.radioshack.com

TAXI CAB COMPANIES
Boston Cab
(617) 536-5010
Cambridge Cab
(617) 494-1300
City Cab
(617) 536-5100
Metro Cab
(617) 782-5500
Town Taxi
(617) 536-5000

RIDE SHARE
Uber
www.uber.com
Lyft
www.lyft.com
Fasten
fasten.com

Clothing Sizes

Women's Dresses, Coats, and Skirts / Sweaters and Blouses

Women's Dresses, Coats, and Skirts						Sweaters and Blouses			
American	6	8	10	12	14		10	12	14	16
European	36/38	38/40	40/42	42/44	44/46		38	40	42	44
British	8	10	12	14	16		32	34	36	38

Women's Shoes

American	4	5	6	7	8	9	10
European	35	36	37	38	39	40	41
British	2.5	3.5	4.5	5.5	6.5	7.5	8.5

Men's Suits, Overcoats, and Sweaters

American and British	34	36	38	40	42	44	46	48
European	44	46	48	50	52	54	56	58

Men's Shirts (this neck size plus sleeve size, 32-36)

American and British	14.5	15	15.5	16	16.5	17	17.5	18
European	37	38	39	41	42	43	44	45

Men's Shoes

American	7	8	9	10	11
European	39.5	41	42	43	44.5
British	5.5	6.5	7.5	8.5	9.5

Children's Clothing

Age	Weight (pounds)	American	European/British
3-6 months	10-16	3-6 months	60
6-12 months	14-21	9-12 months	70
12-18 months	20-28	18 months	80
18-24 months	26-33	2, 2T, 3	90
3 years	31-38	3T, 4, 4T	100
4-5 years	37-48	4, 5	110
5-6 years	45-56	5, 6, 6X	120
6-8 years	52-64	7, 8	130
8-10 years	62-80	9, 10	140
10-12 years	75-95	11, 12	150

Metric Conversions		
In day to day life, the US does not use the metric system. Here is a way to help you convert from metric units:		
If you Know:	**Multiply by:**	**To Get*:**
ounces	28	grams
grams	.04	ounces
pounds	.45	kilograms
kilograms	2.2	pounds
fluid ounces	30	milliliters
milliliters	.03	fluid ounces
teaspoons	ª5	milliliters
milliliters	.2	teaspoons
tablespoons	15	milliliters
milliliters	.07	tablespoons
cups	.24	liters
liters	4.22	cups
pints	.47	liters
liters	2.1	pints
quarts	.95	liters
liters	1.05	quarts
gallon	3.8	liters
liters	.26	gallons
inches	2.54	centimeters
centimeters	.39	inches
feet	.30	meters
meters	3.28	feet
miles	1.61	kilometers
kilometers	.62	miles
acre	.40	hectare
hectare	2.47	acre
Centigrade	9/5(C) +32	Fahrenheit
Fahrenheit	5/9(F-32)	Centigrade

* approximately

Index

Related Publications by The Interchange Institute

Newcomer's Almanac: A Newsletter for Newcomers to the United States
To continue learning about life in the US, subscribe now to Newcomer's Almanac, an 8-page monthly newsletter, written by the Executive Director of The Interchange Institute, Dr. Anne Copeland. Those who have moved to the US for work, school or personal reasons have found the blend of practical tips and thoughtful analysis of American culture a lifeline during their transition. Purchase the optional English Practice Worksheet to turn the newsletter into both a cultural and language tool.

Understanding American Schools, Fifth Edition
This valuable book guides newcomers from around the world through the challenges of understanding the US school system, from pre-school through high school. The Fifth Edition includes the latest statistics, web sites, and international comparisons, and a discussion of the new and sometimes controversial role of the federal government in overseeing education in the US.

In Their Own Voice: Intercultural Meaning in Everyday Stories
A collection of stories written by people who have moved to the United States from another country and culture. In the authentic, personal, everyday moments portrayed here and the commentary that accompanies each story, we gain precious access to the thinking and action behind the value differences that reveal themselves at work and in our daily lives.

Hello! USA, 6th Edition
This classic book has helped over 15,000 newcomers make a smooth and informed entry into the US. The Sixth Edition includes updates of every URL and telephone number, plus pages and pages of brand new material on getting connected on line, registering for school, searching for a home, banking, shopping, cooking, finding medical care and more.

A Smooth Beginning:
20 Suggestions to Help Your Family Feel Settled in a New Country
A 26-page workbook and guide to the emotional and social aspects of moving to a new country.

Global Baby
Tips to keep you and your infant smiling before, during and after your international move.

About the Authors

Karen Rudnick holds a B.S. in Organizational Behavior and a Master's Degree in Applied Management. Her professional emphasis is cross-cultural management. Rudnick was the Managing Director of Savoir Faire, Inc., Lexington, MA, a consulting firm specializing in multiple aspects and challenges of acculturation and international relocation for employees and their families. Rudnick is also a certified English as a Second Language instructor and has designed training programs for tutors of English speakers of other languages. She is a sought after speaker on cultural issues and cross-cultural management matters.

Anne P. Copeland, Ph.D. is Director of The Interchange Institute, Boston, MA., as well as an organizational consultant and a licensed clinical psychologist, specializing in individuals and families who move from one culture to another. Formerly, she was Associate Professor of Psychology at Boston University. She conducts research on individuals and families who relocate to new countries, and writes and speaks frequently about this research.

Helenann Wright was Director of International Education Services at Savoir Faire, Inc., Lexington, MA, where she specialized in the development of programs for people from the United States moving internationally, and for international expatriates and their families moving to the United States.

About The Interchange Institute

The Interchange Institute is a not-for-profit organization focused on the impact of intercultural transitions on individuals, their families, and the organizations for which they work. The Institute conducts research, offers seminars, produces publications and training materials, and provides consulting services to international newcomers, their organizations, and their host communities, recognizing that change and insight on both sides facilitates smooth transition.

For more information, contact us:
info@interchangeinstitute.org
www.interchangeinstitute.org
(617) 566-2227

The
Interchange
Institute

Anne P Copeland, Ph.D
Executive Director